2/12

The Southern-Fried Preacher ℠

Musings from a Made-in-America Minister

Harold Bales

Harold Bales

MINX MEDIA WORX

www.minxmediaworx.com

First Printing, October 2011
Printed in the United States of America

ISBN 978-0-9847144-0-7
Library of Congress Control Number: 2011940888

Harold Bales, The Southern-Fried Preacher
Visit my website: www.thesouthernfriedpreacher.com

Cover design   Donnis Minx
Interior design   Debra Harless

Cover photos   Joye Ardyn Durham, Gingko Tree Gallery
& Author photos   128 Broadway St.
                      Black Mountain, NC 28711
                      (828) 669-7721
                      www.artistwithcamera.com

Published by   Minx Media Worx
                      7401 Battlecreek
                      Corryton, TN 37721
                      (865) 687-5388
                      www.minxmediaworx.com

For individual sales, go to the author's website or contact the publisher.
For quantity sales, contact the publisher.

_In Praise of ...

"Whoever said there can be wisdom in wit surely must have been speaking about Harold Bales. From 'Amazing Grace' to 'Talking About Gizzards,' Harold finds both the humor and God's vision for us in every situation. This book is a treasure and will bring joy, comfort and inspiration to all who read it."

Dr. Norris Frederick
James A. Jones Chair of Philosophy and Religion
Director, Center for Ethics and Religion
Queens University of Charlotte

"Harold Bales' vision of Hades does not include fire so much as frowns. 'One of my nightmares is that I will die and go to heaven only to discover that God is as humorless as some Christian folk I have known,' said Bales. 'To spend eternity with a dill pickle would be...well...hell.'"

Ken Garfield
Former Religion Editor of "The Charlotte Observer"
Author of "So Go On Sing"

"That Harold chose to place the Iva Lee story near the beginning – well, that just plain makes it special, because it's really the foundation of everything he writes. He values people and never hesitates to spend time with them, to laugh and cry with them, and to celebrate what each soul has to offer.

"I can't wait to hold this book in my hand and re-read the stories I've loved over the years, while discovering those I missed along the way. Whether the message is wise or humorous, profound or light-hearted, it is sure to offer a good start to every day."

Marty Folsom
Western NC Conference United Methodist Church
Graphics/Webministry Coordinator

Contents

_F_or Judy

best person, wife, critic, editor and friend
for me forever

$\mathcal{P}$reface

Through the years, I have written and edited several books. All are out of print now. But folk often encourage me to do another one. Mostly, I think, they are just trying make an old man feel loved. I do feel loved. And I appreciate that.

Finally, I weakened under the constant nagging of my beloved Judy. I think she has a sincere belief that somebody might want to read this stuff. There may also be an unconscious desire on her part to make me sit down and do something that keeps me from being underfoot all the time.

Most of the pieces included here were written over the past twenty years and have appeared in newspapers and magazines. Chosen randomly from many hundreds of possibilities, I have edited them for book form, creating a sort of sampler. The pieces are also arranged in a somewhat random order. I want readers to be able to read a snippet here and there — whenever the mood to read strikes. Nobody should read much of this at a single sitting … I'm not sure what the consequences of an overdose would be. It might not be a pretty thing.

I selected these for this book because they survived the big crash. I once lost over 2000 pieces in a computer crash. I took that as a sign from God that they deserved a dignified burial. I hope these will turn out to have been worth keeping.

These pieces were also selected because they made me feel good emotions when I read them again. Good emotions are important to me.

Who needs bad emotions? I can't think of a good reason to revel in bad feelings. I'm a positive guy most of the time and I don't worry much. After all, what's to worry about if you have confidence in the character of God? And I do.

I believe whimsy and wit, candor and honesty, love and laughter are important parts of life with God. I know that some folk disagree with me on this. I have talked with God about this and have been assured that, eventually, this issue will be taken up with those folk.

I can't put this project to rest without thanking all who have listened to my preaching, laughed at my endless yarning, read what I have written and practiced what I have preached for half a century. I especially thank the dear people who endured me as their pastor over the years: Cedar Springs and Union Chapel, in Athens, TN; Unity and Valley Head in Cleveland, TN; First Broad Street in Kingsport, TN; First UMC in Gastonia, NC; Central UMC in Asheville, NC; First UMC in Charlotte, NC; and currently, Trinity in Kannapolis, NC. These are all United Methodist Churches I dearly love.

I have enjoyed writing every word of this stuff. One of my editors once told me to call it "material" instead of stuff. Speaking of editors, I thank my friend Andrew Warfield, editor of the *Lake Norman Citizen* where my column appears weekly. Check their website or my own www.thesouthernfriedpreacher.com for the latest stuff. Who knows? It would be just my luck to win the Nobel Prize for literature and need to do another book next year.

Harold Bales
October 2011

The Magic of Southern-Frying

A magical transformation takes place when something ordinary is "Southern-Fried." A cold, limp, lifeless chicken is to a Southern cook like a blank canvas is to an artist, waiting for the master to bring forth a masterpiece. Entire cookbooks have been written about the culinary execution of said fowl. But if a cook wants her diners to truly smile and squeal with delight when presented with their Sunday supper, she'll get out the big iron skillet, the flour and special spices, and she'll Southern-fry it.

Perhaps before our friend Harold Bales sits down at his computer to create his own Southern-Fried delicacies, he sneaks into the kitchen, gets one of his wife Judy's aprons from the drawer and ties it around his waist for inspiration. How else does he magically transform the simple ingredients of words and thoughts into heart-warming, sidesplitting tales that make his readers smile and squeal with delight? Maybe his inspiration comes from a "Higher" source. Or perhaps his computer is sitting in a big iron skillet and he dabs a little Crisco behind his ears before his fingers touch the keyboard.

When Harold brought this book project to us, we immediately said "Yes!" We knew it would be fun working with him and it has, in fact, been beyond our imagined delight. He has honored us with his kindness, authenticity and generosity. We have discovered the reason he is respected and beloved by the multitudes who call him friend, pastor, teacher, neighbor — even rabbi (he prefers "Your Splendorship"). Harold's hallmarks — twinkling eyes, earthy wit and old-soul wisdom — touch the heart, allow love to flow and life to be embraced as sacred.

After feasting on the stories of "The Southern-Fried Preacher" you'll feel full, satisfied and maybe even magically transformed. This is one "fried food" that is not only good for your health — it will warm your heart, stimulate your mind and tickle your innards.

Enjoy,

Donnis and Debra
The Southern-Fried Editors

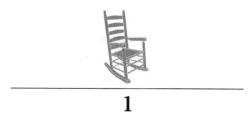

1

An Ode to Okra

I don't know, it may be a hillbilly thing, my yearning to be a song writer. I am, you know, by birth and inclination an Appalachian hillbilly. You might think of me as your melodious yodeling yokel.

Through the years I've written a few songs. The only one that achieved much notoriety was "An Ode to Okra." It was about 30 years ago and I was driving on Interstate 85 when the inspiration swept over me. I pulled over on the shoulder of the highway and wrote down the words lest they escape me and be lost forever.

We Methodists were in the process of publishing a new hymnal at the time. I tried to get it included but failed. I wouldn't have expected it to become one of the great hymns of the church. However, I think it had more soul to it than a few of the things that did get in. I keep hoping that maybe the Episcopalians will put it in their next hymn book. Here's the way it goes:

> *Thou much-maligned by foolish folk,*
> *The suave, the chic, the mod—*
> *Remember thou art nobler yet*
> *Than they, dear humble pod.*

At least no fast-food empire yet
Hath tried to make a bundle
By franchise plunging thee dear one
Into the junk-food jungle.

In skillet and in stewpot now
Where knowing cooks all put thee,
Exult thou soul-food; take a bow,
I love thee grand ol' okree!

2

*M*emorable Iva Lee

The four-year-old child saw her grandmother's false teeth soaking in a glass of water. She said to her mother, "The tooth fairy will never believe this!"

I once was pastor of a wonderful woman named Iva Lee Jarrett. She was past 90 years old when I first met her and was a joy to behold. She had thin, wispy white hair. She peered through very thick glasses. She had a sea-to-shining-sea smile that must have been congenital. And she had one tooth in that wonderful mouth. The tooth fairy had paid many visits to her house. Iva Lee lived in a retirement home and was confined to a wheelchair. I saw her frequently in my pastoral rounds.

I often found Iva Lee with a large-print steamy romance novel in her lap and a plastic cup of wine in her hand. Until I met her, I never knew that such novels were available in large-print editions. I knew the Bible was printed that way for folk with vision problems but this was a shocking discovery for me.

Iva Lee would often offer me a drink. I would say, "Oh no, dear. I would be in trouble with the Bishop if he were to learn I've been over here drinking with you, a single lady." (Iva Lee had been a widow for many years.) She would smile that toothy smile and, as if to shock me, say, "I would *looove* to get you in trouble with the Bishop."

I always looked forward to seeing her because she had a hobby that I have found somewhat common among older women. She loved to tell ever-so-slightly risqué stories to her minister. A few years ago a prestigious Eastern university published research indicating that as some men grow older they experience some shrinking in a portion of their brains. The result is a loss of some of their sense of humor. I've noticed no such phenomenon among women.

I have decided that a sense of humor is the beginning of true wisdom.

On her 94th birthday I went to the party to help Iva Lee celebrate. As we sat eating cake, she turned to me and said, "I have a story for you. A young woman about my age was driving her red convertible down the highway with the top down." (Now get the picture. Iva Lee was creating a picture of herself in this story.) "And," said Iva Lee, "suddenly a big ugly frog jumped into the car on the seat beside her. The young lady reached over and patted the frog on the head. She said, 'My, what a handsome frog you are.' Suddenly the frog turned into a handsome young man… and she turned into a motel!"

If you don't think that story is funny, may the Lord have mercy on your shrinking brain, heart and soul. I have decided that a sense of humor is the beginning of true wisdom. Iva Lee had all things in proper perspective. She made long life appealing despite her physical limitations as she grew older. She cheered everyone who knew her.

Soon afterward, Iva Lee died. At her funeral I tried to capture the essence of her personality in her eulogy. I told the story she had given me on her 94th birthday. Her family applauded! Later they crowded around to express their pleasure at knowing that she had been close enough to her pastor to revel in such stories with him. We all left smiling and imagining that she was, at that very moment, regaling the ultimate minister of us all.

So there you have it, my latest harangue in my crusade against the heresy of humorlessness. This week take a tip from the elders like Iva Lee Jarrett: Lighten up, laugh a little and live on emotional tiptoe. Remember the message on a bumper sticker: "He who laughs last, thinks slowest!" And in a similar vein: "They who don't laugh, don't last!" ✦

3

The True Southerner

I was following a very large sports utility vehicle and noticed the driver was a youngish woman. I thought to myself, "I'll bet she has young children and needs a vehicle like that to carry her kids to ballet lessons, soccer practice and all-American things like that." Then I noticed a bumper sticker that said: *Honk if you love Jesus.* I thought, "She could carry a whole crowd of youngsters to Sunday school in an auto like that. She is a religious person. I like this woman already."

Then the traffic slowed to a stop and I honked. She didn't even look over her shoulder to see who loved Jesus and was honking. She just stuck her left hand out her window and "shot me the bird." I thought to myself, "Child care is tough these days for young mothers. Jesus would understand. After all, he did say: 'Suffer the little children....' I'll wager the young mother was suffering when I honked the horn. Grandfathers suffer lots less when the kids get rowdy. We should be driving the kids around and giving their mothers a break."

Rev. Ray Robinson from over in the Smoky Mountains sent me some insights into how to recognize a true Southerner. He says, "A true Southerner would never assume that the car with the flashing turn signal is actually going to make a turn. Nor would a true Southerner ever scream obscenities at little old ladies who drive 30 mph on the freeway. You just say, 'Bless her heart' and go on your way."

Ray says only a true Southerner can point out to you the general direction of "yonder." He or she knows the difference between "right near" and "a right far piece." He also knows that "just down the road" can be one mile or 20 miles.

Measurements of distance and time are clues to "Southernness." Only a true Southerner knows when "by and by" is. And who else knows how long "directly" is? As in: "I'm going to town. Be back directly."

True Southernness is less about geography and mostly about relationships.

Perhaps the best indicators of true Southernness are the foods that characterize the South. Only a true Southerner knows how many fish, collard greens, turnip greens, peas, beans, etc. make up "a mess."

You may be a true Southerner if you know instinctively that the best gesture of sympathy for a neighbor who's got trouble is a plate of hot fried chicken and a bowl of cold potato salad. If the neighbor is in real trouble you know to add a bowl of banana puddin'.

Speaking of pudding, you know you are in the North Carolina Piedmont if you find liver pudding on your menu. I confess that after living here 20 years I still can't bear the thought of liver in my pudding. Give me bananas or persimmons but leave the liver out of my pudding.

True Southerners know that grits come from corn and the way to eat them is with lots of butter but never with sugar and milk. An even better way to eat them is with country ham and redeye gravy. Of course, if you eat them that way all your life, you will eventually die. At least that's what our doctors tell us. However, I've already outlived several of my doctors. Anyhow, who doesn't eventually die?

A true Southerner says "sweet milk" and "sweet tea." "Sweet milk" means not buttermilk. "Sweet tea" means it is so sugary your tea crawls off the spoon. And even babies know "Gimme some sugar" is not a request for the white, granular, sweet substance that you find in the little bowl in the middle of the table.

True Southernness is less about geography and mostly about relationships. Put one hundred Southerners in a room and most of them will discover they are related, if only by marriage. We make friends while standing in lines. We don't stand in queues. We do "lines" and when we're "in line," not "online," we talk to everybody. And true Southerners pass along wisdom like my friend Ray Robinson does.

The best thing about true Southernness is that you don't have to be born to it. All you've got to do is live into it. And remember that a true Southerner goes bird hunting instead of "shooting the bird." ✦

4

*T*he Funeral

The telephone rang late on a Saturday evening and a woman's voice said, "You don't know me but I have a terrible problem. My father died earlier today and I am calling to ask if you will conduct his funeral. He was not a member of any church and has no minister. My mother is a church member but they have a new minister at her church and she doesn't like him. She refuses to allow him to do the honors for Dad. So I am trying to find someone acceptable to her. Will you do it?"

Then she said, "I need to warn you, I have a sister who is a heavy drinker. She is also an atheist and can be very rude and aggressive. We never know how she will behave when she is drinking — which is most of the time. She is threatening to prevent any kind of religious service for Dad. You just need to be forewarned."

Well, it was a bit of an unusual request but I understand these things. I agreed and asked for a meeting with the grieving family for the next afternoon to plan the service. I tried to reassure her that I had dealt with almost every circumstance that I could imagine and that she should not worry about her sister.

The next day I sat down in a room at the funeral home to meet the family. The widow, the children of the subject in question and a few other family members had gathered. I wanted to learn as much as I could about the deceased.

It was an awkward moment since I had never laid eyes on any of them. However, I was a pastor with many years of experience. I began by asking a leading question: "What, would you say, made him the kind of person he was?" There was a long, uncomfortable pause. I surveyed the room and saw nothing but blank stares.

Finally the deceased's wife broke the painful silence. "Well," she said, "I never understood him. We were married more than 50 years and I don't know why he was the way he was. Within two weeks after our wedding, I knew he was a bitter man. He never changed throughout all these years."

This comment broke the ice and a vigorous debate broke out about Dad. The argument centered on whether he was a person of religious faith. Some members of the family, eager to put the best possible spin on things for the minister who would be conducting his funeral, insisted Dad was a believer. They cited a few times when he had attended church through the years — mostly weddings and other special occasions.

Someone mentioned he had built an addition to one of the churches in town. The deceased was a building contractor. The widow seemed to recall a somewhat religious comment he had made many years earlier but she was uncertain what it was. A son-in-law remembered that the old gentleman had a very elderly sister who was a nun confined in a nursing home in a faraway state.

Then the special daughter spoke up, "He most certainly was not a believer. He was an atheist just like me. We used to walk together down at the track around the high school football field. Then we would go to the neighborhood tavern and have a few drinks together and talk about things. Often we'd talk about religion and he didn't want anything to do with it." Then she said, "I don't want any more of this religious talk. And I don't want anything of a religious nature said at his funeral." She looked directly at me and said, "If you do, I will stop you and set the record straight."

To further complicate matters, the sober sister also mentioned to me: "We will be bringing the twins, our young children, to the funeral." I received that thought and made my preparations.

The next day, as the family entered the packed chapel at the funeral home, I realized how ill prepared I was — for the three-year-old twins. Two tousled little terrors broke away from their docile parents and joined me as I stood behind the pulpit. As I began delivering the invocation, the little rascals went under my robe and grabbed my legs. Their parents made no move to retrieve their children. When I finished one of history's fastest prayers, I opened my robe, took a boy from each leg and placed one under each arm. They were squirming and squealing like joyful greased piglets as I walked into the congregation and presented them to their parents.

I had resorted to taking my chances and saying a few words about God.

The boys beat me back to the chancel! This time they noticed the coffin resting in front of the pulpit. They began to drum with their hands on the hardwood. In that moment, I made the pragmatic decision to leave them alone so long as they were not bothering me. I was pretty sure the deceased inside the coffin was undisturbed. Since nobody else seemed to care much for Dad anyhow, maybe this was some kind of poetic justice. As I walked to my seat, I pondered the parents who seemed indifferent to the whole scene. What newfangled book on parenting had this young couple read anyway?

The soloist was a rather stout lady and wore a black dress decorated with colorful flowers. As she began singing, the twins realized that attention had shifted to her. So, here they came to the pulpit where she stood. As they had done with me moments earlier, they dove inside the draperies. This time, instead of my robe, they crawled under her flowery dress! She grabbed the sides of the pulpit; her knuckles whitened as her falsetto voice rose. She never faltered as she plowed ahead through the song.

I never realized before just how many verses there are to "Rock of Ages." On the third verse, she made a bad mistake. She spread her feet to steady herself, making an opening whereby the boys were able to climb between her legs. It was then that they discovered her half-slip ... and yanked it down around her ankles!

Friends, I could not leave this brave lady in such desperate straits. I reached down and began to unravel two wriggling boys from around her legs. It was almost like an exorcism. She sang while we wrestled. Eventually I managed to snatch victory from the jaws of defeat! And, once again, I delivered the twins to their parents.

When the service came to an end, I was exhausted and drenched with perspiration. As I stood beside the open door of the hearse awaiting the coffin for the trip to the cemetery, I looked up and saw that previously mentioned special sister who had warned me against any religious remarks I might make. I had not been able to come up with very much good to say about the deceased. However, I had resorted to taking my chances and saying a few words about God. I braced myself and waited as she charged across the lawn. Whereupon she threw her arms around me and gushed, "Oh that was the most wonderful funeral I ever saw!" I breathed a sincere prayer: "Thank you, Jesus!"

I tell this story with some anxiety because a few of the principals are still living. But many of them are younger and in better shape than I am and I don't think I'll live long enough to wait until after they are gone. Hopefully they won't ever see this book. I just want to arouse in y'all some sympathy for the poor parson who will someday eulogize you. Please, leave enough of a legacy to remove all doubt as to your core commitments. The preacher will bless you — even if the Almighty doesn't. ✦

5

Waffle House Woes

Trouble! We've got trouble right here in our town! I hear echoes of Meredith Willson's classic, *The Music Man,* announcing trouble in River City because a pool hall was threatening corruption of the town's youth. In our town the villain is not the game of pool. Shucks, these days we've probably got pool tables in some of our churches. And it's not our youth who are at risk. No, my friends, we're all victims! The American way of life is under attack!

Recently I made my regular morning stop for breakfast at the neighborhood Waffle House. I've been pulling up to Waffle House counters and enjoying the usual scrambled eggs, sausage, grits, toast and coffee for about as long as they've been in business… and practically every morning for the last ten or so years.

On this notable morning I was informed that a new company edict required me to add juice to my order. I quickly learned I had the option to refuse the juice but that I would still be charged for it. Other annoyed customers near me were getting the same news. Waiters seemed embarrassed at having to serve as enforcers. It seemed strange to me that I could no longer order what I wanted without paying for something I didn't want. Isn't this like taxation without representation? Is this a new and possibly virulent form of culinary extortion? What has happened at

Waffle House to cause them to junk that historic principle of American capitalism: the customer is always right? Obstinately, I declined the juice and obediently paid for it anyway.

Over the next few days I pondered this challenge to our treasured principles. The increase in the price of breakfast was not the big issue. The trouble was the way this "Southern icon" (that's what Waffle House calls itself on its Website) is now treating its customers. Here is a company that has taken great pride in its ability to innovate. This is a company that advertises it knows how to prepare hamburgers 22,022,096 different ways. That's 22 *million*, folks!

On the other hand, this creative company is now able to sell a traditional breakfast only by charging for orange juice whether the buyer wants it or not! Friends, we are creatures of habit. It's hard to change our taste habits for something as frequent and regular as breakfast. We are doubly snared now. First, by our eating habits; second, by our formerly beloved and trusted breakfast spot!

As time passes, I continue to ponder this. The main thing I'm learning is just how stubborn I am. I notice that instead of almost daily trips to my old stool at the Waffle House, I climb up on it only two or three times per month now. It just goes to show that even a "Southern icon" had better not cross a stubborn, old Southern-Fried preacher.

> *E*ven a "Southern icon" had better not cross a stubborn, old Southern-Fried preacher.

A rational onlooker might say, "It's only a dollar. No big deal." However, to a cranky Southerner like me, that's like the Texan saying the Grand Canyon is "just a hole in Arizona" — which reminds me of the tale about the Texan who was traveling in South America. He looked down into a live volcano and exclaimed, "It looks like Hell!" The tour guide said, "I declare, you Texans have been everywhere."

The Waffle House has every right to run its business any way it wishes. However, I run my own business any way I wish too. The Waffle House website says that Rosie O'Donnell, Britney Spears and assorted other celebrities have eaten in their restaurants. I guess I'll miss my chance to cozy up to the counter with them when they come to my town. Alas.

Footnote #1: I wrote this piece more than ten years ago. On the morning after it appeared in my local newspaper I walked into the Waffle House. The waitresses and cooks gave me an ovation, then served me what they all already knew I wanted for breakfast, picking up the tab themselves! I loved that bunch.

Footnote #2: Since that incident, more than ten years ago, I moved to another town. I don't know what the Waffle House juice policy is anymore. I don't believe I have eaten at a Waffle House more than three or four times now in all those intervening years. It's a Southern-Fried shame.

Footnote #3: I still miss the Waffle House. But a Southern-Fried customer's gotta do what he's gotta do! ✦

6

Keeping Perspective

Perspective-keeping is the most important life skill I know. I have learned this in my many years in the ministry. Well-meaning church members have taught me this.

I once went to a new parish assignment where, on my first day on the job, I was called by a prominent member of the congregation. She telephoned me at 6:30 in the morning to give me a list of things she thought I should do that day. At 10:00 that night she called to check and see if I had done them all. This pattern continued day by day until on the fifth day at the evening reporting time, I replied "no" to each item on her list. I had done nothing that day that she had directed me to do. She was shocked, asking, "Well why not?" I replied that nothing on *her* list of priorities that day managed to outrank anything on *my* list that day.

The parishioner never called me again with a "to do" list. We became the greatest of friends. She was old enough to be my mother and we adored each other. Years later when I gave her eulogy, I spoke as lovingly as ever I had at any of the over 1,000 funerals I've conducted during my ministry. She unwittingly taught me to keep things in perspective and to set priorities.

An anonymous wise person recommends the "epitaph test" as a way of maintaining perspective in a world filled with pressures, choices, dangers, challenges and opportunities. When faced with a tough nut to crack, ask: "Is it important enough to be chiseled on my tombstone when I die?" If the answer is yes, think it through carefully, then get busy and do something about it.

Wouldn't it be awful if you had this carved on your stone: "Here lies Jack. On Thanksgiving Day he dropped a leg of turkey in the lap of his father-in-law. May he rest in peace."

Most of us learn what matters most as we grow older. Aging and experience makes getting and keeping perspective easier. Here are a few insights from some old geezers like me. (1) I started out with nothing and I still have most of it. (2) It's hard to make a comeback when you haven't been anywhere. (3) If God wanted me to touch my toes, he would have put them on my knees.

My friend, Martha Hudson Springs, wrote some random thoughts upon turning 87 years old: "Buy a season ticket? I don't even buy green bananas. My bridge partners are special. We can laugh with each other over our silly mistakes. I still have some friends who don't seem to mind repeating what they say when I don't hear. There are some advantages in being deaf. I don't hear all the noises from the apartment above me. I think twice before getting up from a chair. Is my getting up really necessary? It is a major accomplishment when I can make up my bed without getting into it. I thank God for my life. I thank Him that I can laugh. I thank Him for the love that surrounds me from my wonderful family and friends."

Most of us learn what matters most as we grow older.

Martha is in Heaven now and enjoying perfect perspective. This is perhaps the most important skill in life. It's a spiritual discipline that helps people of religious faith avoid the heresy of underestimating God. ✦

7

A Prayer: After 9/11

On September 20, 2001 I had the privilege of being the guest Chaplain of the Day for the U. S. Congress. Congresswoman Sue Myrick had made arrangements for this several months earlier — long before the horrific events of September 11. Who could have imagined that I would be giving the invocation for the session of Congress just nine days after almost 3,000 persons had perished in the attacks on our nation at the World Trade Center and the Pentagon?

Here is what I said to God on that morning at the opening of the joint session of Congress:

"Eternal God, when we lift our eyes to spacious skies we know that you are there. When as if two lightning bolts slice hotly through the high places and plunge us by the thousands into molten, crushing caverns, we know that you are there.

"When heroic spirits, roused to action, steer a chariot meant for evil to the right and make a crater of courage in the rich soil of freedom, we know that you are planted there as a seed, the seed of life. When wild barbarians spur their murderous winged mount into the encampment of those who serve when called to liberating strife — we know that you are there.

"And when representative forces of freedom meet to do their civilizing work, grant, O God, not only your blessing on their work, but grant your presence there. So, please God, bless this House and those within it that through its actions and by your presence here, justice, mercy, love and peace may come to reign in every house upon this earth. Amen."

During that day I did what the Chaplain of the Day does. I visited with many members of Congress who wished to speak with me. It was a somber day. We talked about faith in these troubled times. I learned that there are many people of faith among our leaders and that they relate to each other across political party lines. They pray with each other and share mutual concerns.

That evening, President Bush addressed the joint session of Congress, the nation and the world. As the Chaplain of the Day, I had the privilege of being present on the floor of the chamber to hear his speech. It was an electrifying moment of national unity. My entire day had been filled with wonder and awe at the sense of common purpose I had observed among members of Congress. Partisan rivalries had been pushed aside to accommodate love of country and resolve to find an appropriate response to an attack on America and her ideals.

When the day was done, shortly before midnight, I stood on a balcony of the Capitol Building and watched lightning bolts stabbing the dark night sky amid ominous storm clouds rolling violently. A flag, illuminated by lights, flew in the strong winds. All the while, the Washington Monument, bathed in floodlights, thrust upward like a defiant white sword, joining, it seemed, the natural elements in rebellion against the forces of anarchy in this world. Years later, now, I'm offering up the same prayer. ✦

8

ℳmazing Grace

A friend over in Tennessee told me a story about a handyman who owned a dog named Mace. Mace was a dandy dog except for one weird, annoying habit: he loved to eat grass. And he ate vast quantities of grass. He could intimidate a Weed Eater with his voracious appetite for grass.

One day the handyman lost his wrench in some tall grass while doing an outdoor job. He searched and searched but was unable to find his lost wrench. As darkness began to fall, he decided to give up the search for the evening and resume it in the morning.

When he awoke the next morning and stepped outside, he discovered that his dog had eaten all the grass in the yard. Lying there, where he had lost it, was his wrench in plain view. As the grateful worker walked over to retrieve his wrench, he said to his dog, "Amazing Mace, how sweet the hound, that saved a wrench for me."

I don't think that is a true story but I like it anyhow. I have known a lot of smart dogs. We once had a little Pekinese named Benny. One day as I drove into the driveway, one of our sons was waving his arms, frantically trying to prevent me from running over Benny. He was an indoor dog, but on this afternoon he was playing in the driveway. The warning was too late. I ran over him just behind his rib cage.

I could not believe the little thing was still alive. I picked him up gently, put him in the seat beside me and drove immediately to a nearby animal clinic. I fully expected him to die before we arrived, but he did not. He just lay there looking up at me with those huge brown eyes. I could read his mind. "Why," he was asking, "did you do that to me? I'm such a little dog and this is such a big car."

I have never been so remorseful about anything in my whole life. I tried to console myself by remembering that I had never known Benny to be playing outdoors before. How could I have expected him to be in my path? Also, I was driving very slowly and coming to a stop when I ran over him. And, I was more distracted than helped by my son's waving. None of my rationalization helped ease my conscience as I looked into those liquid eyes.

Three days later I went back to the clinic to get Benny. Amazingly, he had not only survived, he was doing well and ready to come home. The doctor handed him to me tenderly. "He is very sore. Be careful with him."

As I laid Benny in the seat beside me I noticed he was bent into an L shape where the tire had mashed him. "Don't worry," said the doctor, "Benny will straighten up in time." Then he handed me a small bottle of pills. "These pills are a stool softener. We don't want him to be straining until he is healed. We have already given him a dose today."

I drove toward home grateful and relieved that Benny had survived. Still he looked up at me with bewilderment and suspicion. Suddenly he stirred and struggled to stand. He climbed between the two front seats into the back of the car. I could not see him but I could hear him. First he was down on the floorboard, then he was up in the seat. Busily he sniffed out every inch back there. Then he was quiet. Finally he returned to the front, lay down on the seat beside me and did not move again.

Soon I began to smell an unmistakable odor wafting up from the rear of the car. I pulled the car to a stop, opened the back door and discovered that Benny's medication had moved him to action. Having explored all other options, he had relieved himself in my favorite cap. It had been poised in the back seat for such a moment as that.

Benny slept serenely the rest of the way home. I could read his dreams: "I paid you back, didn't I, big guy?" So, I ask, how smart is *your* dog? ✦

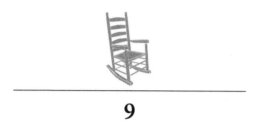

9

Talking About Gizzards

One of my favorite pals is Dr. Joel Krugler. He is a retired business executive and physicist who with his beautiful wife, Nayfee, has come to live in Cornelius, NC. Joel's mind never rests. Since he came south he has been on a constant quest to learn all things Southern.

So when I mentioned in a recent column that I get "soggy around the gizzard…" in reference to patriotism, Joel started Googling to find out what I was talking about. He wrote to tell me his search eventually led back to your devoted scribe. I had used the term in a column last Thanksgiving. He found plenty about gizzards but nothing about "soggy gizzards" except my lone reference. So he wrote me about it and also made a gentle caution about my having reused this old term. Well, as you who have written me know, I always answer my mail.

"Dear Joel, Re: the gizzard stuff. I can't claim much originality for anything. However, I do believe I am the originator of the "soggy" reference. The gizzard is, insofar as I am concerned, a foul but necessary part of the fowl. Many people like to eat fried gizzard of the chicken. Not I, most emphatically! As you know, the gizzard contains small pebbles swallowed by the chicken. This gravel helps grind the corn and seeds the chicken eats. Therefore it contributes to the development of the drumsticks, which are only marginally better to eat. (Personally, I am a breast man.) So the gizzard is a hardworking and essential part of birdly anatomy, worthy of respect if not gastronomy. Therefore I have thought it gallant to repeatedly afford the lowly gizzard a seat of Southern sentimentality — hence "soggy around the gizzard." Your epistle to me has inspired me to feature the gizzard and other fowl references in my column for this week.

I get soggy around the gizzard...

"However, I will now turn to a discussion of my proclivity for plagiarism. I have long held that all originality and no plagiarism makes me a dull writer. Sadly, I have come to the realization that American literary life has arrived at such a sorry state that I am forced to plagiarize myself. Having been caught in this ethical transgression, I am considering suing myself for fraud. I will not try to weasel out of this lapse. Basketball legend Charles Barkley once claimed about something said in his autobiography: "I was misquoted." No, I am a standup guy. I will be held to account. While I am taking this matter under advisement and I ponder whether to bring suit against me, I make a solemn promise to all my loyal readers. Until this matter is resolved and I am fully vindicated, I will not, under any circumstances, read this stuff I am writing any more. I am herewith beginning my search for an experienced defense attorney."

Well, dear friends, I'll let you know if anything ever comes of this. I will close this extra-crispy communiqué with the oldest fried chicken joke I know. As a preacher who has helped countless chickens enter the ministry, I feel honor-bound to keep this story alive.

A city feller was driving to Raleigh one day when he saw what he thought was a game rooster speed past him like a shot out of a rocket. Moments later, it happened again. Soon he spotted a farmer leaning against a roadside fence. He stopped and told the farmer what he thought he had seen and asked if it were possible. "Shore it is," replied the farmer. "My son is going to school over at the Community College where they are trying to develop a chicken with three legs. They figure that because people love to eat drumsticks, if they can produce more drumsticks per chicken, we'll all get rich. You saw two of them chickens." The traveler asked, "Well, how do they taste?" To which the farmer replied, "We don't know. We ain't never caught one yet!" ✦

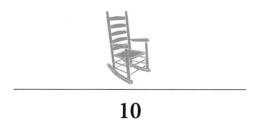

10

The Pompous Preacher

It's as cold as whiz today. And there are snow flurries in the higher elevations, as the breathless weather people call the mountains. Forecasters are predicting rain and snow down here in the lower elevation by mid-week. Of course some of y'all have lots of snow where you live. I have to remember that many of you live outside Dixie. In fact, some of you won't thaw out until August — just in time for next winter.

A while back I telephoned some friends up in Asheville, Sandy and Stan Holt. They had just had their electricity restored. It had been knocked out because of a snowstorm. Sandy told me how their grandson had been snowed in with them. While the power was out they tried to light the house with candles. However, little Nathan kept going around singing "Happy Birthday" and blowing out the candles.

Stan told me about the lady who, upon being told by her pastor that he was moving to another parish, began to weep uncontrollably. Finally she paused to take a breath and he said, "Now, now, don't cry. I know you don't want to see me leave, but I'm sure your new pastor will be a wonderful preacher and a fine person. You will soon come to love him as you have loved me."

It is usually unwise to put pastors on pedestals.

The mournful weeper wailed, "We've had five ministers since I've been a member of this church and every new one has been worse than the last!"

This reminds me of the story about the minister who showed up for his first sermon to the congregation that had called him to be their new pastor. He threw back his shoulders and announced in a pompous and instantly annoying voice, "My dear, dear friends, it gives me great pleasure to announce to you that the Lord Jesus, in His infinite wisdom, has seen fit to send me here to be your pastor."

Over the next few weeks and months, this pastor succeeded in revealing what an arrogant and irritating twit he truly was. Weeks turned into months of frustration and the members of the congregation, resigning themselves to their ill fortune, winced and bore it. Then, one Sunday, the pastor announced to the congregation, "My dear, dear friends, a year ago the Lord Jesus, in his infinite wisdom, saw fit to send me here to be your pastor." Then, adding a dramatic tremor to his voice while elevating his pompous posture, he said, "Now the Lord Jesus has seen fit to call me to be the pastor at another church."

The congregation, upon this announcement, spontaneously rose and with one voice began singing "What a Friend We Have in Jesus!"

I love ministers. Even if I weren't one — I'm a United Methodist minister — I would still love and admire ministers. Of course, all of us parsons have our shortcomings. Usually we are at least as aware of our foibles as our parishioners are aware of them. Hence, it is unwise to put pastors on pedestals, but mostly we are dedicated and sincere servants. I've been a minister 47 years, and I think it is harder now than ever before to be one. I hope you've got a pastor and that you occasionally tell that pastor how much you appreciate her or him. Try it. It might make your pastor speechless. On the other hand, it could cause a 20-minute response complete with a request for an offering, a closing hymn and a benediction. ✦

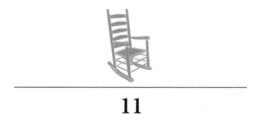

11

*T*ouch Each Other Lightly

I recently wrote about the 50th anniversary for my wife Judy and me. I was in an impish mood when I wrote that piece. Today I want to be a little more serious about romance. I'm an old romantic at heart and I'm proud to confess it. So here is my little meditation on the fine art of life.

The most important things we do in life we do as amateurs: being born, discovering love, getting married, having and rearing children and dying. There's wildness in all these things. Pulse-pounding, breath-stopping, wild-eyed scary, exhilarating, expanding life — these things we do as rank amateurs.

Because of the wildness and mystery of love, sages and singers of songs have never lacked material for their vocations. Diogenes, the Greek philosopher, said, "I have seen the victor subdue all contenders at Olympus and be thrown on his back by the glance of a girl." Rumi, the 13th-century Iranian mystic rhapsodized:

> "Never too many fish in a swift creek, / never too
> much water for a fish to live in. / No place is too small
> for lovers, / nor can lovers see too much of the world.
> Let the lover be disgraceful, crazy, / absentminded.
> Someone sober / will worry about events going badly.
> Let the lover be."

Gwendolyn Brooks has written about being in love:

> "To be in love / Is to touch things with a lighter hand.
> In yourself you stretch, you are well."

What is a marriage but the wedding of these two — the wildness and the wellness? It is one of the ironies typical of classical spirituality that in lightly touching another in love, we ourselves are stretched out and made well.

I have often thought about the principle of reciprocity when pondering love with a light touch. This principle is as venerable as love itself. The Christian expression of it is off the lips of Jesus: "Whatever you wish that others do to you, do you even so to them: for this is the law and the prophets." (Matthew 7:12) He spoke from his Jewish tradition.

> The Talmud puts it: "What is hateful to you, do not do to others. That is the entire Law; all the rest is commentary" (Shabbot, 31a).

> Other great religions echo this conviction. The Buddhist says: "Hurt not others in ways that you yourself would find hurtful" (Udana-Varga 5,18).

> The Confucian says: "Surely it is the maxim of loving-kindness: Do not unto others that which you would not have them do unto you" (Analects 15,23).

The Muslim says: "No one of you is a believer until you desire for the other that which you desire for yourself" (Sunnah).

So, then, how do we amateurs make a marriage of the wildness and wellness of love and lovers? I say, as one who has marked 50 years of marriage, touch the one you love lightly. When we touch each other lightly, we are both made whole. Poet Anthony Machado says:

"Look for your other half
who walks always next to you
and tends to be who you aren't."

The happy marriage is one in which both persons understand that what each needs is a mate who tends to be who their beloved is not. ✦

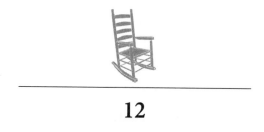

12

*H*eart Surgery
Published: 1992

A strange thing happened on my way to my last deadline for this divine column; I stopped in at Carolinas Medical Center for quintuple bypass surgery. But there is more of a story and I've even been accused of doing this entire stunt just to get an angle for a column. Here's my story and I'm sticking to it.

A few days ago I went to see my physician, complaining that I thought I was developing asthma or some other respiratory ailment. I was having trouble breathing, especially while walking and talking. To make a long story short, it turned out I was experiencing congestive heart failure. What a shock! A series of tests indicated I have apparently had several heart attacks over time without realizing it. Having searched my memory, I cannot find a single clue indicating any trouble with my heart.

Over a few days of testing, the doctors found I have massive problems. To sum it up, it appeared that more than 80 percent of my heart was blocked and dead. Bypass surgery cannot revive dead heart tissue. They also found that my heart was working at only 16 percent of normal capacity. It looked grim indeed.

But the Lord blessed me with some great physicians who did not give up on me. They kept working and eventually presented Judy and me with a glimmer of hope. Sanger Clinic surgeon Dr. Larry Watts theorized that there might be more life left in my heart than appeared. He suggested the possibility that my heart might be "hibernating" rather than dead and that some bypasses might awaken the slumbering muscle.

One thing I learned throughout this adventure is that you need physicians you can trust to be perfectly candid with you, and Dr. Watts was that with us. He explained that because of the weakness of my heart, there was a greater than ordinary chance I would not survive the surgery. Furthermore, there was no guarantee the surgery would bring the desired result. Finally, there was no short-term prospect for survival without surgery. I could expect only a few months to live.

This information, of course, made the decision to proceed easy for us. We set a date for the surgery that would allow me a few days to get my affairs in order. I did not, however, get the luxury of that. Soon, a trip to the emergency room, a few hours of preparation, and I went to sleep in the care of God, a team of heart experts, nurses, family and friends.

Dear friends had assured me they would take care of my family. My children surrounded me with expressions of love. Our teenage daughter, Susannah, who was away in New York on a mission trip, gave me by a long-distance phone call the last words I remember hearing before I went under the anesthesia, "Daddy, I will sing you through your surgery. I love you." I later learned she did that in a New York City center while holding the hands of a mentally retarded senior citizen who could not communicate normally but who loved music. She sang "You Are My Sunshine."

I am home now, less than two weeks after surgery. I'm doing great. I expect a long and healthy future. And I am very clear about the following: I am living evidence of a miracle. I am so filled with gratitude that I am not able to talk much about it yet. I have dissolved in tears several times while writing this. Many of you have been through similar experiences and can identify with me. I'll be back in my pulpit soon.

Meanwhile, keep this guy with the heart of a bear-awakened-from-hibernation in your thoughts and prayers! And this word to the wise: If you've got anything sleeping in you — wake it up! ✦

13

The Funniest Things Happen at Church

Some of the funniest things happen at church. Recently I was with a bunch of my relatives and we began to tell tales about funny things that have happened at church. My favorite Baptist preacher and I were swapping yarns. His name is R.C. Harless, and he is my uncle. He lives near Knoxville over in Tennessee, is in his elder years now and mostly retired.

His daughter Denise asked, "Has Daddy ever told you about his first church?" Then she began the saga. In her father's first church there was a woman who had a big bunch of children. She sat with her children on the front pew, always there with her nursing babies. This mama fed them the old-fashioned, *natural* way. "Nursing" was common back in those days. It fell out of fashion for a while but has experienced resurgence in more recent times. Anyhow, that's how this mother did it, and sometimes she did it while Daddy was preaching.

"The mother never covered herself when she started to nurse her baby. Daddy's neck began to get red about right here." Denise brushed her hand across her neck, just under her chin, and continued, "His face would start turning red. Then his eyes would begin to move upward toward the back of the opposite side of the church."

Here I am with my uncle and mentor, R.C. Harless

We family members began laughing as the word picture began to emerge. The Reverend Daddy sat quietly, smiling serenely as his daughter continued, "Sometimes the mother nursed two babies at the same time. Daddy's eyes would go higher and higher. Sometimes the babies became full and content and lost interest. But mama never noticed. She sat there listening intently — hanging out on the front pew, so to speak."

At that point another daughter, Becky, chimed in and said, "That's when Daddy's eyes would cross!" The reminiscences were pretty much over at that point. We all exploded into gales of laughter.

There was an old song popular in rural, Southern churches in the mid-20th century, "Gimme That Old-Time Religion." I don't know whether incidents like this inspired the songwriter or not. Lots of funny things happen on the front pew where the rest of the congregation can't see what's going on. However, those things can certainly challenge the concentration of the preacher!

Sometimes the concentration of the congregation is challenged as well. Once, somebody shot out a little piece of the stained glass window in a church where I was the minister. We learned about the small hole when a bird flew through it into the 11 o'clock service.

The congregation saw it first. The bird began to circle above my head as I preached. I was oblivious to it. Soon the congregation could not maintain its composure. Some attendees baffled me by giggling for no reason apparent to me. Others maintained sober faces but their eyes betrayed their distraction. Older folk were horrified that the bird might descend to land on the most inviting landing field — my reverent, bald head. The young folk were hoping the bird would dive-bomb my gleaming target or, better yet, fire a liquid shot right inside my halo. In a few seconds I spotted the foul fowl intruder and held a hymnal over my endangered pate. The book was open to my least-favorite hymn. The benediction came early that day.

I tell y'all this to encourage you to attend church on Sunday. There are many important spiritual reasons to do this. Also, something really funny may happen there too. It's rare, but these things are gifts of God too. Why? Only God knows. ✦

14

$\mathcal{O}$n to the Bible

I love the Bible. Lots of folk who are fond of the Bible like to say, "We need to get back to the Bible!" Of course we know what they mean. They want us to be more obedient to the timeless truth of the scriptures. I'm for that too, but I like to challenge folk to go **on** to the Bible too. There are tons of treasures there that are often overlooked. I like to encourage people to read it through the eyes of a detective: Read between the lines.

$\mathcal{I}$ like to urge people to reread the beloved old stories with mature eyes.

Look for clues hidden there that can enrich our understanding. Look for new insights going forward in addition to holding to the old verities.

I have discovered that some folk who love the Bible still rely on their memories of the great stories of the Bible from hearing them in their childhood. I like to urge people to re-read the beloved old stories with mature eyes. Look afresh at the details. For instance, what kind of fruit did Eve offer Adam in the story of creation? Lots of us think instantly of the apple we see in many artists' portrayal of the scene. Actually the Bible doesn't say what kind of fruit is offered. It just says "fruit." It may have been a persimmon or a kumquat … or a fig. Who knows?

I know it's a minor point of no consequence whatsoever. But it is interesting how many images stick in the public mind that really aren't in the Bible. Here's a tip: If you hear something that sounds vaguely biblical but can't find it in the Bible, check in the *Farmer's Almanac*. You may find it there. Or check classical English literature; it may be there.

Sometimes when I preach, I like to start my sermon with a little Bible quiz. I want to challenge the listeners' Bible-reading imaginations. I want to encourage them in their Bible studies. Now, dear readers, just to tease you a bit, here's a Bible quiz someone gave me.

Question: What kind of man was Boaz before he married Ruth?
Answer: He was Ruthless.

Question: Who was the greatest financier in the Bible?
Answer: Noah. He was floating his stock while everyone else was in liquidation.

Question: Who was the greatest female investor in the Bible?
Answer: Pharaoh's daughter. She went down to the bank of the Nile and drew out a little prophet.

Question: What kind of motor vehicles are found in the Bible?
Answer: Jehovah drove Adam and Eve out of the Garden of Eden in a *Fury*. David's *Triumph* was heard throughout the land. Also there must have been a *Honda* because the apostles were in one *Accord*.

I'll pause a moment to allow all the booing and hissing to subside. Now, I failed that quiz too, despite my many years in the ministry and two graduate degrees from a very fine American theological seminary where I became educated far beyond my intelligence. They didn't teach any of that kind of stuff in school.

My quiz for you this week is the following question: Do you know what they call ministers in Germany? *Answer*: German Shepherds. Sorry about that! When I get on a roll, my mind floods with old jokes!

I'll close with a simple idea to help as you read your Bible. When you see a word or comment that raises a question in your mind, put a "**?**" in the margin. This will remind you to do a little further study on that point. If you see something that is a new insight that you have not seen before, put an "**!**" in the margin. If you see something you ought to do, put a "**^**" in the margin. And if you see something that you ought to toss out of your life, put an "**X**" in the margin. Remember, it's okay to write in your Bible. A well-marked Bible is a well-read Bible. It honors God when we pay close attention to the Word. Good Bible reading! ✦

15

*T*he Cost of a Dog

I read recently that it costs approximately $6,500 dollars to raise a medium-size dog to age 11. It got me to thinking about Little Bit, our miniature poodle. We got him several years ago as an economic measure. We had been given a beautiful black mixed-breed dog by friends. He was a medium-size dog, playful and friendly. However, even as a puppy he had a monstrous appetite.

The trouble was that he didn't only love puppy food: he had a particular taste for lawn chairs, table legs and the lumber out of which our deck was built. He once ate a baseball bat on a weekend. He loved to chew and play. I can't for sure say he digested any of these items; he just "processed" them. When Midnight, as we named him, began to gnaw away the doorframes of the house, I knew our domestic tranquility was at stake. Given time I could see him running up a tab that would require us to calculate his cost in board feet.

I had a friend who owned a farm in a neighboring county where I knew Midnight would be able to frolic and gnaw on timber to his heart's content. So I worked out a deal and drove out on a Saturday to deliver Midnight to his new home. I then went to a pet shop to bring home a puppy of more modest appetite. That's how Little Bit came to preside over our little suburban spread.

Naming this little jet-black bundle of curls was quite a challenge for us. We considered lots of possibilities. I favored a French name for him. He is a poodle, after all. I suggested *Oui Oui*, which met with cries of derision by my wife and our five-year-old daughter. "What kind of name is that — Wee Wee?" they wailed. Finally we compromised on Little Bit.

The second challenge was to avoid stepping on him. He was so tiny I often mistook him for a wadded-up black sock lying on the bedroom carpet. Eventually he grew enough and moved enough that I was able to distinguish him from my socks. I was also moved by compassion for him and started picking up my socks instead of tossing them on the floor.

As Little Bit began to grow we discovered he could not be trusted to be an indoor dog. Mother Judy insisted he was dumb. I argued that his problem was not a lack of intelligence but, rather, an inclination toward procrastination. This, coupled with an unbounded exuberance, caused him to forget to go — until in the midst of his playful activity he would discover that his hydraulic system had been pushed beyond its limits.

So Little Bit became an outdoor dog. He loved this. As he grew, he became a testosterone-driven machine. He terrorized the squirrels in our yard. They began building their nests above the 50-foot mark in the trees, despite our never seeing him charge more than three feet up the tree trunks in pursuit of a furry rodent.

He also developed a fearsome bark for a creature so small. One morning around four a.m., our doorbell rang and I opened the door to two serious but friendly policemen. Little Bit had awakened the entire neighborhood, except for us, with his yelping. With daylight I discovered a large, terrified possum on our back porch. I think the barking had caused the frightened marsupial to try to crawl inside her own pouch!

Through the years he has calmed down a lot. He barks a little but doesn't persist like he once did. He used to lurk near the gate looking for an opportunity to dart through an opening. Once his greatest pleasure was to escape our clutches and hang out in the neighborhood. He doesn't do much of that any more.

As he grew, he became a testosterone-driven machine.

Little Bit's coat is turning gray and he's mostly a consultant now. He and I sit around and chat a lot these days. I can't chase him much anymore. The fun of escaping our yard has almost disappeared for him. He wishes I were a better match for him like I used to be. I do too. But he is patient with me. I told him today how grateful I am that he's such a little thing. I know it's not going to cost much to care for him until he becomes 11 years old. Even if it does, it will be worth every penny. And if all else fails, I won't object to him eating a little lumber now and then. ✦

16

*T*he Shave

I received a note asking if I would send another copy of a recent "Southern-Fried Preacher" column. It seems the first copy got involved in an "unfortunate mulching incident." The report of this mulching incident aroused my curiosity about the potential uses of this blessed blurb. People tell me they copy it and share it with Sunday school classes and other groups of friends. Lots of folk tell me they pass it on to relatives and family members.

I imagine some insomniacs use it to get some sleep. Do you recall the unfortunate Eutychus who was sitting in an open window of a second story room one night while the Apostle Paul was preaching? Paul preached on into the night and Eutychus finally got sleepy and fell out of the window. It was just a rumor, I know, but I understand that Paul, fearing that reports of his long-windedness would spread among the populace, started a rumor of his own. I have it on good authority from a source, who wishes to remain anonymous, that Paul went around town for days on end claiming that Eutychus was reading "The Southern-Fried Preacher" when he dozed off and plummeted to the cobblestones below.

I don't put much stock in rumors myself because I start so many. You can use this column however you wish.

I got the following story from two minister friends, Bill Simpson via Bob Baldridge. The Baptists among you, dear readers, will understand it instantly. So if you don't get it at all, please share it with a Baptist who will explain it to you.

After 20 years of shaving himself every morning, a man in a small Southern town decided he had shaved enough. He told his wife that he intended to let the local barber shave him each day for the rest of his life. He put on his hat and coat and went down to the barbershop, which was owned by the pastor of the town's Baptist church. The pastor's wife, Grace, was working that day, so she gave him a shave. She shaved him and sprayed him with lilac water and told him, "That'll be $20." He thought the price was a little high, but he paid her and went on off to work.

The next morning the man looked in the mirror and saw that his face was as smooth as it had been when he left the barber shop the day before. Not bad, he thought. At least I don't have to get a shave every day. The next day his face was still smooth. Two weeks later there was not a trace of a whisker.

This was utterly baffling to him, so he returned to the barbershop to inquire how it could be that his shave was so long lasting. "I thought at the time that $20 was a bit high for a shave," he told the barber's wife, "but you must have done a great job. It's been two weeks now and my whiskers still haven't started growing back."

The serene expression on her face did not change. It was as if she had expected his return visit and his question. She responded, "You were shaved by Grace and once shaved, always shaved." ✦

17

The Southern-Fried Daughter

I never claimed to be impartial when it comes to my children and grandchildren. And I know you think yours are the brightest and smartest in the world. But I'm here to tell you that my Southern-Fried daughter, Janice, is my favorite domestic wit. She has always been a kind of down-home-Erma-Bombeck-sort-of-gal.

From time to time she gets inspired and dashes off a letter venting on Southern culture. Often she writes about food and cooking. Here's an excerpt from one of her letters:

> "I decided a few years back that there are few things more pitiful than a really bad southern cook. Let's face it, every Southern cook has a Momma or Mamaw who was 'the best cook in the county.' Or so the myth is told. I beg to differ. There are not enough counties in the South to account for all those best cooks. Also, there are lots of cooks in the South who just can't cook, and I'm one of them.
>
> "Take cornbread, for instance. How hard can it be to bake cornbread? For me, it's virtually impossible. My friend Mary has told me 100 times how to make cornbread, but the lessons never take. And don't get me started about gravy. Making good gravy requires

a 'knack' and I don't have it. I get pots and pans from family members every Christmas because they know my tendency to burn things up in the kitchen. I can make anything ethnic — Greek, Italian, Spanish. I just can't cook Southern. This is a shame because I live in Nashville, Tennessee.

"I do, however, know a few things about Southern cooking. Take okra for example. Everybody knows the only proper way to cook it is to fry it. Of course, we make allowances for cooks in Louisiana who have their own boiled version because they also give us that really good Cajun crawfish.

"*Poke sallet** is another Southern delicacy that people not from this region cannot understand. They ask, 'How can something that grows in the ditch alongside Highway Route 22 taste so good?' I can answer that question with two words: fatback! Maybe Momma and Mamaw were right and I should just stay out of the kitchen. I guess I'll stick to doing the laundry and leave the cooking to the real pros. Incidentally, Mom, you're about out of detergent!"

The truth is, Janice is a very good cook. All the women in our family are fine cooks. But I can see how Southern women are under lots of pressure. They are, perhaps unfairly, *expected* to be very good cooks. Maybe this is true in all subcultures.

A few weeks ago, Janice sent me a letter that she wanted me to pass on to the editor of this column. I'll just include it here:

"My name is Janice White but you can call me the Southern-Fried Preacher's daughter. Save your jokes about preacher's daughters. Believe me, I've heard them all! Y'all know my dad, but maybe not my mom. Mom is strong and can be tough if she thinks Dad is going out for a paper and then finds out he has been sighted at Baskin-Robbins. Hell hath no fury!

"Dad is the best man that I know. Mom is the most forgiving woman that I know. That explains why they have been married so long and put up with me for so long. Daddy is my favorite man, but you know what they say: 'Behind every good man there is a woman telling him to stay out of the ice cream!'"

What's not to love about such self-deprecating humor, especially from someone you love more than life itself? What would life be if it weren't for the love between a father and his daughter? Or between a mother and her daughter? Or between parents and their sons? I don't even want to think of what a joyless world it would be. And don't get me started on grandchildren!

And you want to know something great? You don't even have to have blood kin to enjoy the pleasures of family. Just look around and find or make a friend whose well-being you can come to care more about than your own. Cook up some grits and greens and okra and feast on friendship. It will be like manna from the Lord for you as you journey toward the Promised Land.

A postscript: Moments ago, after my writing the above, my wife, Judy, and I received word that our dear Janice has died. It is her 45th birthday. After a decade of very poor health, she has gone to be with God. We are leaving for Nashville with tears but also gratitude for the love that sustains us all. See you here in this space next week. Pray for us. ✦

Poke sallet is an old, traditional Southern dish made from the cooked young leaves of the wild pokeweed or pokeberry plant. The word "sallet" comes from Middle English and refers to a mess (another Old or Middle English term) of greens cooked until tender. Sallet is cooked greens; salad is uncooked greens.

18

A Different Kind of Tears
Published: September 2007

Recently I wrote about the wit of our oldest child, Janice. Shortly after I finished that column, we received word that she had died. So I added a postscript to my column, and my wife, Judy, and I began the long, sorrowful trip to Nashville to be with our grandchildren.

Janice died on her 45th birthday, having become a widow just the year before. She had suffered greatly from a rare illness for more than ten years. A few months before she died, she was told that she had nine months to live and that her condition could not be cured. This situation caused an even more special bond between her and me.

Five years ago I was told I had a few months to live and nothing could be done to fix my bad heart. Janice and I had many conversations about this over these last few months of her life. She was brave and hopeful. She never lost her wit, although she was in and out of the hospital repeatedly. Her core character showed through as her condition worsened.

As a child and youth, she was always fighting for the underdog. She loved church work projects to help the poor. Her first job was driving a van to take handicapped, poor and elderly people to their appointments with doctors. She loved to cook for friends. Recently, a friend brought her a crate of overripe bananas. Despite her weakening health, she made

30 loaves of banana bread to distribute to friends. When we gently teased her about this facet of her personality, she wrote: "God helps those who help others. I do." Then she added: "After all, I *am* a Methodist."

We continue to grieve. We are people of faith so we trust in the character of God. As a pastor, I have stood hundreds of times in the presence of death and spoken only of life. I have often preached that people of faith are the people who can laugh in the face of death. Now I am practicing what I have been preaching for more than 40 years.

But we are still grieving. I know this will continue for a while. Eventually it will evolve into other dimensions of emotion. Serenity will come to dominate. Pleasure and laughter will bring joy. Endearing memories will be enduring memories.

My daughter had aged enough that she was becoming the steward of many of our family memories. She loved to ask, "Do you remember...?" Then she would remind me of something said or done during her childhood that I would never have recalled except for her. She recently wrote about the first (and only) time I ever spanked her. She remembered with laughter about her Daddy, "He cried and I didn't."

Last Mother's Day she wrote: "Daddy, do you remember when we used to go to Mamaw and Papaw's every Christmas Eve? Well, I do. Daddy, you and the boys were supposed to load Santa Claus stuff in the station wagon. It was snowy, so it was slow going. All of the luggage was left on the front porch in Nashville. We spent Christmas Eve at K-Mart in Knoxville, buying underwear and toothbrushes. Boy, was Mom mad! But we made it." I had forgotten about that incident from many years ago. That is the kind of thing that ought to be remembered. She was my keeper-of-memories of things that are now among my favorite treasures. Memories are to the past what hope is to the future.

Many of you, dear friends, have experienced these kinds of sorrows and joys. You already know about what I am discovering. When a parent survives a child, it brings a different kind of tears. I don't know anything about the chemistry of tears, but I am an expert practitioner of weeping. I know about the sweetness of crying with laughter and weeping for joy. But there is nothing comparable to the stinging bite of the sobs that flow, when you have regained your breath, upon learning that your child has gone ... even to be with God.

Jesus said, "Blessed are they who mourn. They will be comforted." That is true. That goes for you too. ✦

19

*E*veryone Needs a Rabbi

Early in my ministry, I went to be a pastor in Kingsport, Tennessee. I quickly became friends with Norman Sobel, a merchant there. Our friendship grew very deep.

One day Norman paid me the greatest compliment I have ever received. He asked, "Would you be offended if I were to call you Rabbi?" He is Jewish; I am United Methodist. He explained that the word "rabbi" means "teacher" in Hebrew. This I already knew, but I listened intently as he explained his request.

He said that his late father had enjoyed a deep friendship with the Presbyterian minister there in Kingsport. For many years he confided in him. He sought counsel from him. He trusted him. Out of great respect, he regarded and called the Presbyterian minister "Rabbi." "And," said Norman, "I have not had such a person like my father did. May I call *you* Rabbi?" Thus this preacher became a rabbi.

Now, everybody needs a good rabbi. Through the years, I have come to realize that I now regard my friend Norman as my own rabbi.

Last week I received an email from Norman in which he sent me a blessing for good health. His blessing was adapted from a New Year's prayer by Rabbi Mitchell Wohlberg. The prayer is based on thoughts by Rabbi Jacob Pressman. As you can see, there are loads of rabbinical wisdom and loving sentiment in this prayer. It is full of wit as well. Here are a few excerpts adapted slightly for brevity.

> "During coming days, may you enjoy good health and happiness! May you have a kiss from your beloved, a smile from a child, a warm cozy home with the aroma of good food baking in the oven! May you have a merciful IRS agent, good friends and helpful neighbors! May your computer and your refrigerator both be safe from spam, and may your email bring you only good news and jokes that are not as old as you are!
>
> May you finally learn what it is that you are supposed to eat! Is it more pasta or less carbs? Or less pasta and more carbs? Or is pasta a carb, in which case you can't eat it at all? Should you drink more coffee for the sake of its invigorating caffeine, or should you drink decaffeinated coffee which is healthier and which comes with a choice of artificial sweeteners — one of which causes cancer and the other causes brain damage — I can never remember which?

May your hair, teeth, facelift and your stocks not fall, and may your blood pressure, cholesterol and mortgage interest rate not rise. May the West Nile virus go back to the West Nile where it belongs and leave the rest of us alone.

"May your occupation give you much satisfaction. May it also earn you enough money to send your children through college and graduate school and to support them ever after. May your children and grandchildren receive good reports in school and may you receive good reports also — from your dentist, your ophthalmologist, your dermatologist, your cardiologist, your gastroenterologist, your podiatrist, your urologist and ultimately from your God. Whenever it rains — and it will — may you have an umbrella!

"May you follow the teachings of the Torah with love, and may this year be happy, healthy and prosperous for you and your loved ones."

Now isn't that a blessing to lift your spirits? It is reassuring to me to have my own personally appointed rabbi, Norman Sobel, who is on speaking terms with God in my behalf. And I am honored to be a rabbi to Norman. We men and women should all be so fortunate as to both have and be rabbis to each other. ✦

20

$\mathcal{E}$lectricity

A traveling salesman approached the humble farmhouse after pausing at the barnyard and scooping up a handful of aromatic dust in a small paper bag. It was a sweltering summer morning, not a wisp of wind about.

As he walked up onto the porch he took note of the house. It was a typical rural home, timeless in its simplicity. It had never worn a coat of paint. A porch swing hung motionless on chains beside the front door. Who knows how long the little house had been home sweet home to generations of farm families?

The salesman rapped on the frame of the screen door. Soon the lady of the house appeared and opened the door. Before she could utter a word, the salesman grinned broadly and leaned inside the door. He then dumped the bag of dust he had brought from the barnyard on the floor in front of the homemaker. He said, "Madam, the fine vacuum cleaner I am about to sell you will pick up every bit of that or I will eat what is left on your floor."

A mischievous smile spread slowly over her face and she said happily, "Well, come on in. We ain't got no 'lectricity out here!"

I was born in that kind of house. One night shortly before he died, I sat with my dad in his hospital room and we reminisced together. He told me about Ol' Doc Jenkins, as he was affectionately known in our rural community in East Tennessee. Dad told me how that wonderful country doctor tended my mother during her pregnancy with me. Doc Jenkins came to our house and delivered me on a cold, snowy January morning. My dad said, "He did all that and charged $25 for the whole deal." Then Dad said, "But, son, you've been worth every penny of it!"

I don't remember when it happened but I must have been about four years old when we got electricity at our house. Then, by the time I was 12 years old, we had television. I marvel at the fantastic changes I have lived to see in my short lifetime.

How did we ever get along before we got electricity? How did we cook our meals, make ice cubes, wash and dry our clothes, read at night, run our air conditioners, heat our houses, clean our floors, open our garage doors and operate our computers? How was personal hygiene possible? How did we shave our whiskers? How did hairy people run their blow driers? How did we brush our teeth? What about entertainment? What powered our satellite dishes and our VCRs?

I don't think I'd want to go back to the good old days. Just think of all the appliances that would be left cluttering up our houses and contributing nothing for lack of electricity. It would be a waste.

It would be like the time the picture tube died in my Grandmother Harless' television set. She was too frugal to have it replaced. So for months she sat in front of it, looking at a blank screen and listening to the sound as if it were a radio. Eventually she arose from her chair, tossed her sewing aside, turned off the sound and said to nobody in particular, "Television ain't worth a *x&*%* without the picture."

Of course, that's the truth, as was most of what I remember Mamaw saying. Most of what I remember about the good old days was the good old people who knew and told the truth. ✦

21

The Prom

Sometimes something so good and beautiful happens, it makes you want to believe in God. Recently, 30-year-old David overheard someone talking about a school prom. He asked his mother, the Reverend Millie Orbison, "Mom, have I ever been to a prom?" His question broke his adoptive mother's heart because David has serious physical, as well as mental, impairment. And no, he had never been to a prom.

David's sister, Pam, heard about her brother's question and it cut right to her own loving heart. She determined that David would finally have the chance to go to a prom. She and their mother Millie got busy and began to dream. They recruited a few volunteers to help. Pam's church contributed a modest grant and a place to hold the prom. Sister Pam and parents Millie and Jerry pitched in lots of dollars.

Finally, on a Saturday afternoon, David and more than 150 men and women with similar handicapping conditions attended the first prom of their entire lifetimes! They ranged in age from the 20s to past 50. Some were profoundly handicapped, some were in wheelchairs; all were significantly impaired.

They began to arrive at two in the afternoon. For the next several hours, they underwent a transformation. Volunteer beauticians set up a beauty shop in the church parlor. They worked tenderly to groom the women's hair, apply makeup and give manicures. The women dressed in gowns. The men donned tuxedos.

All this was a first-time experience for these guests of the prom. It was made possible because Pam and Millie had searched every possible source — wedding and formalwear shops — for retired clothing that they bought for eight, ten and twelve dollars per piece. The clothing was a gift to the wearers when the evening was over.

The most touching moment for me was to observe a beautician apply cosmetics to a woman whose face was so badly contorted and disfigured, most people cannot bear the sight of her. All her life she has endured averted eyes. She has never been able to look full in the face of another human being. The volunteer now was only inches away looking full into that face, smiling and putting on lipstick. They were both beautiful!

While the promgoers were being primped and dressed, volunteers were preparing a banquet and the church family life center was being decorated with beauty to rival the finest country club — although it was in a rural church. Volunteers in formal dress served the feast, then the dance began and it was a joy to behold. A stretch limousine picked up promgoers at the door of the building. They were driven slowly 300 yards around the neighborhood and then they went in to the dance.

One woman (I'll call her Mary) was a notable exception to all the other women at the dance that night. She brought her own dress to the prom. Sixteen years earlier, the week before she was to attend her high school prom, Mary was approached by school officials and informed that it would be best if, because of her condition, she did not attend the prom. So she stayed home with the dress her family had bought for her to wear laid across her lap. But on this night, after all these years, Mary finally got to wear that very same dress to an honest-to-God prom after all. Unknown to Mary, her parents stood outside the hall and watched through a cracked door while Mary danced. And they wept with joy. ✦

22

*G*race in Marriage

In 2010, Judy and I celebrated our 51st wedding anniversary together. We eloped right out of high school. We have been married all our lives, and still she loves me. It's an amazing thing. I have teased and tormented her all these years. She has endured my silliness. I began in our first week of marriage to try to make her jealous by pretending to be mumbling the names of my former girlfriends in my sleep. She never mentioned it.

She has put up with all my eccentricities. She has been bombarded by my bad habits all these years. I have been changed by her. However, I have disguised most of the change to spare her the satisfaction of knowing she has reformed me.

Despite all this, the porch light is always on when I get home at night. Except right now. One of the lights burned out last week, and I keep forgetting to replace it. It will be burning again soon. I *am* going to replace it, but only after Judy goes *two* days without reminding me to do it. (It's a husbandly thing, you know.)

My friend Erman Bradley sent me an essay on marriage written by Richard Cabot in 1914. Here's what he said way back then:

> "It is fashionable nowadays to talk of marriage as a contract between husband and wife. This is something

like calling violin music a contract between fiddle and bow. It is not untrue; it is merely foolish. There is a contract in marriage and there is a contract between bow and strings. But there is so much else, that no one in his senses should pick out this subordinate element to characterize the whole."

Back in the old days, the norm was that when the magic had left a marriage, the husband and wife would tend to stick with what they were stuck with. But today is a more "romantic" era and when the wonder wanes, things can become unstuck in a hurry. All it takes for lots of couples is for boredom to set in and they set out — separately of course — seeking their individual bliss.

Have I told you about the couple sitting in the rocking chairs on their front porch? The husband turned to his wife, patted her on her hand and asked, "Dear, do you know what today is?" She replied, "No, what's special about today?" He said, "Today is our 50th anniversary! Why don't I catch that old rooster, you fry it and let's mark the day?"

We have been married all our lives, and still she loves me.

The wife then, with a mixture of weariness and bewilderment in her voice, asked, "Why should we punish that old rooster for a mistake we made 50 years ago?"

At about the midway mark in our marriage and after the untimely death of a friend's wife, I began to reflect on what I would do if I were suddenly single again. I was overcome by a profound sense of gratitude for my wife — for her love and loyalty, her persistent patience with me. It was for me an overpowering parable of the theological concept of *grace* — an experience of one of the main attributes of God. The memory of that moment continues to cause me to try to keep the main thing *THE main thing* in my marriage. You'll have a better and more lasting marriage if you will do that too. ✦

23

*N*aturally

I felt pretty smug about myself on Saturday. We gathered at the Dennis Vineyard, over near Albemarle, for the wedding of Patrick Baldwin and Emily Baumgardner. It was a lovely setting. Orderly rows of lush vines and adorning rolling hills overlooked a gazebo beside an emerald pond. An hour before the outdoor wedding, storm clouds began to gather over the scene. Far away, faint thunder rumbled and summer lightning began to stab the darkening sky. Then large raindrops began to fall — not in abundance, only in threat of a coming deluge. We went into rain delay mode.

After a patient delay, raindrops stopped falling and we decided to proceed. The large gathering of guests began to stroll the hundred yards down the pathway to the white chairs spread over the lawn at the gazebo where I stood for the ceremony. The sky seemed even darker as the wedding party participants began to make the march to the altar. Lightning punched the darkness. Jeff Baumgardner escorted his daughter down the long outdoor aisle. She was beautiful.

Our thoughts shifted from the threatening forces of nature to the bride. Brides have a way of brightening a sanctuary — even an outdoor one. Still, the lightning flashed in the dark grey canopy hanging over the region. I knew what was on everyone's mind. Everyone was filled with anxiety that the wedding of this handsome couple would be spoiled by a cloudburst — to say nothing about the chance that all of them would be suddenly drenched in their summery wedding finery far from shelter.

When I greeted the assembly, the sky was ablaze with a distant light show. Departing from the traditional greeting, I said, "Dearly beloved, if you, like I, have been praying that this marriage be filled with electricity, please stop it now!"

Now, friends, you know your beloved old ministerial meteorologist would not bear false witness about this. The lightning stopped! Right then! That was the last of it! We had a lovely wedding. Soon the sun broke through and drove the clouds away and it was a beautiful day for everyone!

Here's another nature report for you: My beloved and I enjoy sitting on our porch watching birds come and go to our feeders and birdhouse. Last Friday evening, Judy was sitting there when a bird lit on a nearby wrought-iron rail. Moments later the bird flew to another perch closer to Judy. It sat a moment, then jumped to a small table inches from Judy's elbow. Then it hopped onto Judy's shoulder, kissed her on the cheek and nibbled on her ear. The little feathered friend then flew onto Judy's other shoulder and began to pull her hair with its beak. Finally the bird flew away. I thought Judy, in her joy, would take flight too!

On her 45th birthday, our daughter Janice went to be with God. There's nothing that can hurt your heart as a parent quite like the death of your child. The smallest things can trigger big emotions, serve as signs of hope and cause your memories to multiply. Judy said to me, "I named the little bird Janice."

I remembered the incident when Jesus and the disciples were in a boat on the Sea of Galilee. As often happens on that body of water, a sudden, strong storm arose. The disciples were frightened. The Bible says Jesus quieted the storm. The cynic might dismiss that report as a violation of the laws of nature. I leave you to come to your own conclusion about that. But if you are facing a storm or entertaining a little bird, simply say what Jesus said to the storm, "Peace, be still." Naturally. ✦

24

A is Always "A"

One of the most widely read books in the 20th century was a historical novel based on biblical times entitled *The Robe*. It also became a notable motion picture. The author, Lloyd C. Douglas, wrote other works that were especially inspirational to Christian readers.

Douglas once told the story of how he, from time to time, would visit his friend the violin teacher. The little old man had a studio, a small room, in a row of similar rooms where other music teachers taught. Douglas enjoyed their friendship:

> "I liked to drop in on him, for he had a kind of homely wisdom that refreshed me. One morning I walked in and, by way of greeting, said, 'Well, what's the good news for today?'

> "Putting down his violin, stepping over to a tuning fork suspended from a silk cord, he struck it a smart blow with a padded mallet and said, 'There is the good news for today. That, my friend, is 'A.' It was 'A' all day yesterday. It will be 'A' all day tomorrow, next week and for a thousand years. The soprano upstairs warbles off-key, the tenor next door flats his high ones, and the piano across the hall is out of tune. Noise all around me, noise; but that, my friend, is 'A.'"

Musicians, writers, preachers and lots of other folk cultivate images, metaphors, parables, poems and songs that open windows on timeless truths for times when the earth shakes and chaos threatens to consume us. Then some saving image is offered up by a seer, reminding us of a deep truth and bidding us to anchor there. That's what I am feeling the need for during these days and nights of nonstop media coverage from our nation's wars: something to hold onto.

As I write this, I am praying that the wars will be over soon. However, I'm old enough and experienced enough and realistic enough to believe the biblical assertion that we will always have wars and rumors of wars. The "war against war" is one war that seems unwinnable. It is no wonder I take refuge in the knowledge that 'A' is always 'A' in God's musical scale. Could civilized life exist without music? God give us some music!

I am reassured to know that God's alphabet of order amidst the chaos still holds. When confusion rules, serenity evaporates, and it seems all the lettered tiles have been swept off the Scrabble board of life, 'A' still provides a starting point for the reconstruction of words … meaning. Look and listen for the 'A's!

The "war against war" is one war that seems unwinnable.

The current conflict is the prototype of the stereotype of religion-driven warfare. Christianity, Islam and Judaism, lubricated with Middle Eastern oil, provide ideal conditions for political sparks to ignite a firestorm. What an irony that these are the great living world religions that worship the same God. Alas.

How I wish the whole world would embrace the vision of James Michener, another 20th-century writer of historical fiction. Michener, orphaned as a very young child, was adopted and raised by a loving Quaker family. Because he never knew his biological family, the famous author said he was forced to consider the possibility that every man or woman he met was his brother or sister. What a world this would be if we were all so disposed! ✦

25

Tomatoes, Politics and Patriotism

It is not that I'm a really deep thinker, of course, but I do get things on my mind that are hard for me to shake. For instance, I think a lot about tomatoes. Have I told you about my tomato theory? I believe a tomato was the fruit that Adam ate in the Garden of Eden and, according to the Bible story, introduced sin into the world.

I know some of you think it was an apple but the Bible doesn't say what kind of fruit it was. Look it up in Genesis 3. Maybe it was a banana or a fig. It could have been a Georgia peach. Who knows for sure? As for me, I think it was a homegrown, vine-ripened tomato because it was so sinfully good.

Furthermore, I reckon if Eve had offered Adam a modern, store-bought tomato, he would have turned it down flat. Sin would have been avoided. Adam and Eve wouldn't have been kicked out of the garden, and we wouldn't feel so unkindly toward snakes. It's just a theory, of course, but it makes sense to me.

Another thing I think a lot about is politics. I have lots of friends who are excellent, honest, hard-working public servants and politicians. A while back, I was talking to some Republicans who seemed to think the Kingdom of Heaven arrived with the last election. It didn't. And while walking the dog, I spotted a Democrat crouching behind a bush murmuring that the world was coming to an end. It wasn't. A long time ago I discovered that some folk take their politics far more serious than they take their religion. That's okay, I guess, if they would like to spend eternity in Congress. Obviously some do.

A third thing I think a lot about is patriotism. I'm a very patriotic sort of guy. I come by this naturally. My ancestors have served in the armed forces of America since the American Revolution. During World War II my grandmother, Ida Harless, had four sons and two sons-in-law serving overseas all at the same time. Now, if you want to talk patriotism, when you get to Heaven, ask her about it. One of her sons, Bernard, was a jeep driver for General Patton. Another, Paul, was a crewman on the presidential yacht of Franklin Roosevelt. Later he shot down a kamikaze plane in the South Pacific. James, her second son, was awarded two Bronze Stars. My dad received the Purple Heart for terrible injuries received in Europe. I honor those who serve in our military services.

Like most who serve with heroism and patriotism, I hate war. I long for the time when the Prince of Peace will reign over a world without gunfire, bombs and other sounds of conflict. It will take the rise of sanctified patriotism for this to occur. I'm not naïve about any of this. So much of what is commonly called patriotism is anything but holy. Still it is worth praying for earnestly and continually.

Some folk take their politics far more serious than they take their religion.

Bible believers know you can't love God if you don't love your neighbors. It's also true that you can't be a disciple of Jesus if you aren't a peacemaker. Jesus once said, "Blessed are the peacemakers." I wish this were not so complicated to understand and so hard to achieve. But it is what it is. Peace is a product of justice, honesty, piety, fair play, generosity, hospitality, faith, hope and charity. Also, empathy, forgiveness, repentance, grace, mercy… Start wherever you wish and God will cheer you on! ✦

26

*M*y Uncle Paul

My uncle Paul Harless is one of my favorite people in the world. He lives down in North Augusta, South Carolina. He is almost 90 years old. We talk often by phone, spinning yarns and family history. Paul is a great storyteller with an extraordinary past and a perfect memory.

In 1940, at age 19 the young sailor Paul was transferred from service on a U.S. battleship to the crew of the U.S.S. *Potomac* — President Franklin Roosevelt's presidential yacht. It was known as the "Floating White House." For two years he served as Boatswain Mate 3rd class. Almost every weekend the president would come aboard and the ship would sail up and down the Potomac River or along the eastern coast. Although Mr. Roosevelt suffered from polio and couldn't walk, he had great upper body strength and loved to fish from the ship.

Sometimes, before World War II, FDR entertained visiting world leaders — kings, queens and such — with yacht rides. Paul recalls taking the president to a meeting in 1941 with Winston Churchill aboard the cruiser, the U.S.S. *Augusta*. It had been announced as a fishing trip but, in fact, was a secret meeting between the two leaders in which they drafted "The Atlantic Charter."

One of my favorite stories from the memory bank is an incident off the coast of New England during one of the fishing trips. Paul believes this story has not yet found its way into print until now.

While sailing along the coast they spotted a lobster fisherman with a good catch. The president called from the deck of his yacht, "I'd like to buy a bushel of lobsters."

The fisherman yelled back that he would not sell Mr. Roosevelt a bushel of lobsters. Then he said, "I'll give you a bushel of lobsters. I want to be remembered as the man who gave the last Democrat president a bushel of lobsters!" In my imagination, I can see it now: the president leaning back in his chair, huge smile on his face, pipe stuck jauntily in his jaw, roaring with laughter. Paul remembers Roosevelt for his warm, friendly, human qualities.

Conversations with my Uncle Paul brings to mind Tom Brokaw's book *The Greatest Generation*. After two years on the "Floating White House," Paul was assigned to a destroyer for the battle in the Pacific. The U.S.S. *John Rogers* was involved in more raids than any other destroyer in World War II. It received 12 battle stars and in 200,000 miles suffered no personnel losses. A recounting of those experiences has an unsettling effect on ears today as we hear the daily death toll from Iraq and Afghanistan. Suicide bombers baffle and terrorize us all. We are bewildered by the mind-set that prompts a person to take such radical action for what seems to us to be such a senseless sacrifice.

In his papers, Paul has a letter of commendation for having shot down a kamikaze airplane and preventing it striking the ship. It was on May 14, 1945 during the Battle of Okinawa. He was a gun captain, when he jumped behind an unmanned gun as the Japanese plane came roaring in. He shot into the plane and apparently hit the bomb it was carrying. The plane disintegrated instantly. The propeller came off and continued spinning toward the ship. The ship's deck was peppered with fragments of engine parts. The propeller landed on the deck, then fell over the side. And the plane with its pilot tumbled into the sea.

The meaning of kamikaze is "divine wind." The only sense I can make of these things is that some people lose their spiritual way when infused with the idea that they may achieve some kind of eternal bliss by an act of personal destruction. An act of devotion to an Emperor god was, for the kamikazes, a way to gain some measure of godliness for themselves. Alas, there turned out to be nothing divine about that wind.

Now my sons David and Philip have done a neat thing to honor their great uncle. They have made a scale model of the U.S.S. *Potomac*, which is now on permanent display in the museum at the Southern White House in Warm Springs, Georgia. President Roosevelt made more than 40 trips there to soak in the hot waters for relief of pain caused by his polio. His little cottage is preserved just as it was on the day he died there.

David is a master woodworker, but without naval experience. Philip is a naval veteran with a scientific mind. Philip is a stickler for detail and naval precision. David is a perfectionist too. The two of them spent more than 200 hours working together creating the model made of 1/8 inch thick balsa wood planks. It is almost four feet long and very fragile. They began by laying a keel and building the ship much like ships are built in real life. Models of the U.S.S. *Potomac* are very rare and this is the only model ever made by these brothers.

My son Dave, Uncle Paul and my son Philip with U.S.S. Potomac model in background.

Uncle Paul speaks often to veterans, schools and community groups about his naval experiences and his service as a member of the president's crew. He is the only surviving member of the crew and one of a very few persons living today who worked up close with the President Roosevelt. Ours is a family of patriots serving all the way back to before the Revolutionary War. ✦

27

$\mathcal{M}$r. Gentry's Whistle

The young Methodist preacher, Glenn Evans, was pastor of a small congregation in a little rural village. He was also a student in a theological seminary. He commuted to class an hour each way each day. It's a common practice for beginning clergy to receive their education while getting on-the-job training. It's also a unique mission for many small churches — helping train young ministers for their vocations.

On this particular afternoon the student-pastor, still new to his ministerial assignment, stopped in at the village grocery on his way home from school. As he paid for his purchase, the grocer asked if he had yet paid a pastoral call at the Gentry household.

No, he replied, he had not. He knew Mr. and Mrs. Gentry. She was a member of his congregation. Mr. Gentry was not a member. He was a member of the Baptist congregation in the village. However, he was the teacher of a Sunday school class at the Methodist church. The Gentrys were well known and greatly loved in the churches and community.

"Well," urged the grocer, "when you get a chance to visit the Gentry home, if Mr. Gentry happens to be in his rose garden tending his flowers, don't look at the front porch. Engage Mr. Gentry in some friendly conversation. Then let the conversation lag. Mr. Gentry will then begin to whistle. When he begins to whistle, look on the front porch, and you will discover why Mr. Gentry whistles."

The young minister could hardly wait to get home that afternoon. He kissed his wife, dropped his books on the table and excused himself. "I'm going to visit the Gentrys." He walked through the village to the Gentry home. As luck would have it, Mr. Gentry was working in his rose garden. Wearing rough gloves, he was pruning the thorny stems. The pastor, hoping to preserve the surprise, declined to look at the front porch. He greeted Mr. Gentry, who removed his right glove to shake hands. They began to chat as Mr. Gentry put his glove back on and resumed his clipping. After a few words, the conversation lagged.

Suddenly, the old gentleman began to whistle. It was not a tune that he whistled. There was no melody to it. It was just a note, an unwavering tone. When he heard the whistle, the young man finally looked at the front porch to learn the mystery of the whistling. There, upon the porch, sitting in an old-fashioned porch swing was Mrs. Gentry … and she was blind.

Mr. Gentry whistled to reassure her that she was not alone. He wanted her to know that he was just a whistle away from her. He was ready to come to her if she needed him. His whistle was a reminder that she was loved and cherished by the one who had been her loyal companion for so very long.

The novice servant of God stood inside the garden fence as if in a cathedral. He thought he heard a great hymn, "Praise God from whom all blessings flow. Praise him all creatures here below. Praise him above, ye heavenly hosts. Praise Father, Son and Holy Ghost!" ✦

The novice servant of God stood inside the garden fence as if in a cathedral.

28

*M*y Friend Cicero Fudd

My old buddy Cicero Fudd has lived a largely uneventful life. Until recently, he lived out in the country, where he ran a little fertilizer business. He is retired now and has moved into town. He spends lots of time sitting on his front porch, pondering the deeper things of life and annoying almost everyone. Cicero learned he bears the same name as a famous old philosopher. So he sits with chin in hand and furrowed brow and thinks of ways to confound others.

Recently he went to see his doctor for a checkup. After a thorough examination, the doctor told him he was in excellent shape for a 65-year-old man. "Who said I'm 65 years old?" replied Cicero. "I'm 75 years old." The doctor then asked if Cicero's father lived to a ripe old age, to which he replied, "Who said he's dead?"

The doctor asked if he was still living and Cicero said, "Yep, he's 94 years old." The doctor pursued his questioning and asked if his grandfather had lived a long life. "Who said he's dead?" replied my old pal. "He's not only living, he's 110 years old and about to get married." Then the baffled physician asked why a 110-year-old man would want to get married? Cicero said, "Who said he *wants* to get married?"

Last week I found him engrossed in an old book, *The Papers of Samuel Marchbanks*. He shared, "This here's a writer you can put your confidence in. He knows what's what. Listen to this: 'Love, like ice cream, is a beautiful thing, but nobody should regard it as adequate provision for a long and adventurous journey."

Cicero did not know that his wife, Delilah, had walked up behind him as he spoke. "What a feller needs for the long haul is some grits instead of ice cream. Grits has got stayin' power. Delilah is a lucky woman to have a husband whose grits have cooled off rather than one whose ice cream has warmed up."

Well, I thought Delilah would go right off into orbit. She charged around in front of him, thrust a forefinger right between his eyes and let him have it. "You egotistical varmint! Why don't you ever ask me what *I want* instead of always thinking you're so smart?" She was really angry. I don't think I've ever seen her so aggressive. It took Cicero aback momentarily. As Delilah whirled around and stalked off, he muttered that she had become "one of them women's libbers."

"Cicero," I said, "I think you ought to cultivate a little more romance in your life. Delilah deserves more from her marriage than cold grits." He said he reckoned I was right, but it would embarrass him to get, as he put it, "swoony." I encouraged him just to try a little tenderness every once in a while, then reassured him that I was certain his heart was in the right place.

"Speakin' about hearts in the right place," he said, "Sam Marchbanks got to feelin' bad the other day, so he went to a doctor and got X-rayed. Went back a few days later and looked at them pictures hangin' on a rack and lit up from behind. He went into a panic when he saw a long, thin, twisted monster with a hook on each end gnawin' at his vitals. He just knowed he was a goner. It turned out to be a picture of his

What a feller needs for the long haul is some grits instead of ice cream. Grits has got stayin' power.

zipper. That just shows even a picture of a feller's innards don't always show exactly what's what. You can't always judge a cob by its corn."

I could sense that Cicero was beginning to get agitated with me, so I gently withdrew. Maybe a seed was planted in his mind that will eventually bear fruit. I think Delilah's on the right track. I just hope she won't give up on the old geezer. He's got more love in his heart than he knows how to express, and he's got a lot of grit too. He's got the right provisions for a long, adventurous journey. ✦

29

ℰmail Ads

There was a time when one of the best indicators of what Americans were thinking about was *The New York Times* best-seller list. I wonder if that is any longer true. In this world of Internet communication, maybe the best indicator of what preoccupies us is the list of email advertisements left on our computers each day by purveyors of one product or another.

On a recent December day, before erasing all the unread emails from writers I did not recognize, I made a list of topics on my screen. Here are a few of the topics I found. You will note that each was followed by an exclamation mark, indicating the exciting nature of the message.

(1) *"Harold, you can do it!"* I confess I was tempted to open this email to find out what the "it" is that I am capable of doing. I assumed

the sender of the message was standing by, eager to tell me how to do the "it" for a fee. I declined the opportunity mostly because there aren't many "its" that I haven't already done that are worth doing.

Then I came to a section of size-related topics. (2) *"Increase your bust size today!"* I am perfectly happy with my bust. It has been the same size for about 30 years. My shirts all fit. Why would I want a bigger bust? I am not smarter or more popular now than I was before my bust achieved its adult dimension. I'll just keep the bust I've got.

Next in the size-related messages was a promise to (3) *"Increase your penis 3 inches in 22 days!"* Now, insofar as I know, since my mother died 18 years ago, the only people still living who have ever seen this part of my anatomy are my wife and my physician. How can somebody who doesn't even know me make a judgment about such a private matter? And what is magic about 22 days? What would happen in a month or a year? *Delete!*

There was another message that may fit this category, (4) *"Hey guys! Upsize your flies!"* Upon further reflection, I decided to consider that a message about insects. Since I already have an exterminator contract on my house, I didn't need to open that email.

There was a message with a generic size-related theme. (5) *"HGH. Human growth hormones. You need it!"* Maybe I do, I don't know. I have seen ads for growing hair but have always been suspicious — and cautious. When you use something like this, what's to insure *where* the hair will show up or *what* will grow?

The more tempting email was the challenge to (6) *"Lose 32 pounds by Christmas!"* This was tempting, but by now I had begun to grow cynical. Christmas was about three weeks off but *which* Christmas was being referenced? This year's or next year's? These e-commerce shysters are just looking for suckers like me, aren't they?

Then came the inevitable appeal to the universal yearning for youth, (7) *"Start growing younger now!"* I am the eternal optimist but I know this is impossible. I'm not even tempted to open this one.

Finally, I deleted the last and, in some ways, most intriguing message of all: (8) *"Why wake up your wife at night so much?"* I remain totally in the dark about that one.

I don't know what this kind of daily unsolicited Internet communication signifies about modern American life. At the very least it means that there are apparently lots of people who buy what these advertisers are selling. Else, why would the hucksters buy the ads? Go figure. ✦

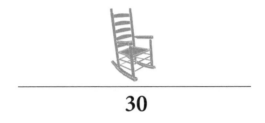

30

*D*udely Papaw

A new generation of writers is emerging in the Bales family. The lead writer is my grandbaby, 14-year-old Megan Bales. She has mesmerizing blue eyes and an arresting wit. About three years ago, and fascinated by hearing her talk about things of interest to her circle of friends, I realized I was out of touch with her peer group. So I asked Megan what I needed to do to become more youthful. She said, "Buy some jeans and start saying 'dude' more often."

Ever since then, I have been working at being *dudelier*. Last week she and I had a flurry of email exchanges. Here are a few snippets from the exchange. (The parenthetical comments are my own.)

> Megan: "Hey Papaw! I was just sitting here bored to salty tears and thought about writing you a not-so-handwritten sentiment. :) I hope you're having a fantastic

evening and that you're feeling better. When my mom told me you went to the hospital, at first there was that feeling of shock and fear. But then about two seconds later I remembered you could kick any illness's metaphorical "booty." Haha. Well luckily it wasn't too serious and you got to go home quickly."

Me: "Hey Megan! I'm glad you dubbed me a 'metaphorical booty kicker.' The only time I ever had an editor censor a word in one of my columns was once when I used the more literal term for 'booty.' :) I can now use this new term and retain my place in polite society. Also, you are the first person to write me and include *emoticons** in your letter. Before this, I didn't even know what an emoticon was." (*A typed symbol that conveys emotion. Example: :-) Looks like a smiley face tilted sideways.)"

Megan: "Awww! I'm so glad to have amused you! You don't know how perfect it was to read your reply at the moment I did. You see, about two seconds ago Caity (Megan's older sister) and I were yelling and fighting about something totally stupid, insignificant and forgettable. In fact I'm not even sure why I was spending my ever-loving breath on it.

"Anyways, I was sitting at my computer, red-faced and huffy, when all of a sudden that catchy little "You've got mail!" animation popped up. My expression eased into a smile as I read your message. And by the end of it,

I had totally forgotten about ol' what's-her-name. Don't get me wrong. I love my sister, but she can be a real 'expletive' sometimes. :) But, of course, nobody in this family can see that. I once told Caroline (Megan's aunt) that and she looked at me like I was Boo Radley (See: *To Kill a Mockingbird*) out from the basement! Everyone thinks she's a precious angel and I'm the troubled one. *Pshh*. That's ridiculous.

"And on that note... I would like to address your dudely studies. Now, at first I wasn't worried. But now, I'm beginning to shake and pee a little like those Mexican Chihuahuas do. I really think you need to step up to the dude plate and really swing! Hit that home run to win the dude World Series! Alright, I think I've taken that baseball analogy a bit too far ... ha-ha. Well, what I'm trying to say is you've been slacking off a bit and it's hurting you dude-wise. Come on! Step it up! I think I'll have to make you an inspirational poster or something... Love ya Papaw!"

What's not to love about a 14-year-old grandbaby like Megan? In another email, she said she likes to say to her friends: "Hey guys, wanna see my mega-culio Papaw?" (Culio is an old rapper.) "And then I just show them your website! Haha. They are all so impressed! Most of their papaws just sit around in the basement looking at war stuff and bootleggin' moonshine. :-) You're so much cooler than them." ✦

Footnote: Megan gave me permission to show y'all this. Maybe, I'll need to give Caity equal time. :-)

31

$\mathcal{A}$irport Security

I feel safer now. I took an airplane trip recently. It was the first time I have flown since I had a pacemaker installed. At the security check-in, I told the checker I had this contraption and was whisked out of line into a more private area where I got a thorough search. I took off my belt, my shoes and my watch. I also took the smile off of my face because, when I stood with my arms outstretched so my body could be patted down, my pants began to fall down.

Now, I'm a manly sort of fellow, so having my pants creeping down in front of a witness is unsettling enough. But being touched all over my body is particularly unnerving to me. The man doing this was very professional, and I appreciated the importance of what he was doing. However, when he examined the soles of my feet, I couldn't resist flinching and laughing. This was not good.

I had already begun to perspire, and I could feel my face flushing. The examiner seemed especially intent. Besides feeling all over my body, he ran the wand all over me searching for metal. The beeper went off when he came to my right ankle. That made no sense. It is just an ankle, for heaven's sake. Then I remembered that I have a little screw in that ankle. Eventually I was cleared and made my flight.

Once I arrived at my destination, I checked into the hotel and opened my luggage. There I found a document atop the contents of my bag explaining that my luggage had been broken open by airport security in order to search it. I had made the mistake of locking it. So it had been entered forcibly. *Then* when I turned my laptop computer on, I discovered that it had been ruined somehow during either the flight or the search.

On my return flight a few days later, I experienced a virtual replay of the initial security check. But I felt safer because of all the attention. It was reassuring to know that airline security is on the job and vigilant. However, since I've been telling this tale, I'm reconsidering. Maybe I'm not so confident after all.

I'm looking at myself in a mirror as I write this. I'm a reasonably honest-looking fellow. I have a gentle look on my face. Every hair is neatly in place. (Well, that may not be an especially impressive indicator of stability.) My eyes have a twinkle that is almost always there, although they are capable of getting beady at times. It is true that I wear a moustache and goatee, but both are white, and I look a lot like the old folksinger Burl Ives, whom some of you are old enough to remember. I don't look like a terrorist. I look like everyone's grandfather! *Good grief!* Why was an old geezer like me getting all that scrutiny at airport security? Are people with pacemakers especially likely to be suicide bombers, wanting to blow up planes? I wouldn't think so. We are mostly especially grateful to be alive!

> *My* eyes have a twinkle that is almost always there, although they are capable of getting beady at times.

I remember looking at all those other people in the airport who walked right on in. I suppose 200 passengers passed through security while I was being searched. Some of them looked like they were perfectly capable of hijacking the plane. As I think back on it, they all looked more dangerous than me … including the woman in the wheelchair. She was old enough to be my grandmother, and they searched her too.

Now that I think more about it, I'm feeling less, not more, confident about airport security. It wasn't me that they should have been searching. All those truly suspicious-looking characters are the ones who should have had to take off their shoes. They are the ones who should have had their bodies touched all over by a stranger — not I, your beloved old Teddy bear. If I ever take another plane trip, I think I will just go barefoot. And if I'm in danger of missing my flight, I may just leave off my britches as well. I don't want anyone to feel frightened around me. ✦

32

The Haircuts

Little Bit and I got haircuts this week. He's one of my best friends, but it costs me a fortune to get him a haircut — $45 nowadays. That's three times what it costs for me. Both of us also get our whiskers trimmed in the deal, though. 'Course, Little Bit has lots more hairs than I do.

To make things worse, he has to get a coif more often than I. Little Bit, as you may remember, is our 12-year-old miniature poodle, and his graying hair grows rapidly and kinkily. The good news is that I won't need another 'do' until after Thanksgiving. I mostly get a haircut just to relax and nap to the hum of the clippers.

Little Bit needed his haircut because of this dangerous heat wave we've been having. We got worried that the little hotdog might have a sunstroke if we didn't take off his overcoat. Oh, he can stay indoors whenever he wants and enjoy the air conditioning. However, he is a conservative creature with traditional values like duty and loyalty. He has a strong work ethic and insists on keeping his rounds as the watchdog of our little yard. Despite the heat, he wants to be out there keeping vigilance against pesky squirrels and a raucous bird or two. I forced him inside in the afternoons this week to cool off. He and I watched cable news reports about terrorist bombings in London and Homeland Security here. He now seems even more resolute about his job. A man's got to love a dog like that.

We wouldn't object if he were to develop a meaningful canine relationship, but there just aren't any Fifi's in our neighborhood.

Little Bit usually gets his hair styled in a sissy sort of way: a fluffy topknot, big whiskers, powder puff on the end of his tail and furry ankles. He has never once complained about this. He knows girls think he's cute, and he has a vague notion that this is a good thing. But I've never had a man-to-man talk with him about such things. His life circumstances have simply dictated a celibate lifestyle for him. So he hasn't brought it up, and I don't really know what I'd say to him if he did.

This time we had him clipped short all over. No puffy hairballs anywhere. He looks as cool as a cucumber, although I did see him staring curiously at his reflection in the storm-door glass. This new image is decidedly manly compared to the way he has always looked before. I wish I could read his mind. We wouldn't object if he were to develop a meaningful canine relationship, but there just aren't any Fifi's in our neighborhood. Plus, he seems totally content with chasing chipmunks and crickets in his little gated domain. I think I'll leave well enough alone.

Our dogs are truly important to us Southern-Fried folk —always have been. In the early days of our history, a pioneer farmer needed a fighter and a hunter in his dog. A watchdog guarded the family and the farm animals. They wanted a dog that could howl down the moon when necessary.

I remember sitting on the porch late at night with my grandfather. We would listen to the hounds barking while leading hunters in pursuit of raccoons and bears over ridges and valleys. He was too old and I was too young to chase with the dogs, but we knew what was happening. Papaw would give a running commentary on the progress of the hunt simply by the sound of the barking. He knew the voice of the individual dogs.

The mascot of the University of Tennessee Volunteers is Smokey, a Bluetick Coonhound. I love the breed: sad-eyed, floppy-eared, uniquely patterned in its markings. What's best about Ol' Smokey is his howling in the dark of the night. It's so deep and rich it can cause the hills to tremble. It'll scare the horns off the devil himself. Haints and boogers flee at its wail.

My son David has such a Bluetick Coonhound. His name is Rufus, and he's a lovable romper. But when he howls … I know I've heard him from ten miles away. I love sweet Rufus and wish you could hear him howl. But I also thank the good Lord that you don't live within 20 miles of Rufus's voice. It's a sound only its Creator and a hillbilly can love. ✦

33

Laughing Through the Tears

Two dear friends died last week. One was Lula Wix over in Asheville. I was minister at Central United Methodist Church in downtown Asheville when I first met her.

When I received word that Lula would like a visit from me, I stopped by her house to see her. Lula was blind and lived alone at home. I knocked on her door and was greeted by her watchdog, Tiffany, a tiny white poodle who took her job very seriously. She planted her feet in a wide stance and barked ferociously at me. Then she bit me on the ankle!

To make a long story short, after I got past Tiffany the sentry, Lula and I became instant friends. Shortly thereafter, when I welcomed her into church membership, I announced to the congregation that even though her dog bit me, still I was allowing Lula to become a church member!

She lived into her 90s. I loved Lula. She loved me. We sat and held hands and talked about deep things. But because of her blindness she was never able to see me. Now this little angel has flown the tug of this world and entered eternity. I used to tease her and tell her how handsome I am. Now I'm counting on her being able to see me with her own new eyes.

Randy Burrows from near Salisbury died. At his memorial service we remembered how I first met him. I was superintendent of the United Methodist Churches in the region at the time. I went to hold a business meeting at the church where Becky, his wife, was a church leader. Randy was noted for not being a member of the church.

Pastor Tommy Conder was a bachelor at the time and not a great cook. So, because there were no restaurants in the rural community, he asked Becky if she would invite us to her house for dinner before the meeting. As he drove me to the Burrows home, he prepared me for meeting Randy. He said, "Randy has been making a fuss about our visit. He has been saying all over the place 'Aaah, Becky has done invited the damned Pope to our house for dinner! She's made me mow the yard and clean up all around here! My neighbors are getting worried about me!'" Tommy got me all fired up about this man whom I was about to meet.

When we arrived at the home, Tommy introduced me to Randy, and I held out my hand for him to kiss my ring. This popely gesture completely flummoxed Randy and rendered him speechless. While he struggled to speak, I said to him, "Randy, if you don't wish to kiss my ring, I have another location I can offer you!" Folks, before that night was over, Randy and I were friends for life! The next Sunday he became a member of Bethel United Methodist Church where we met last week and commended him to God forever.

Ah, two great friends have taken their places among the saints who from their labors rest. I got to know them both in memorable ways. They left marvelous memories that have filled me and their friends and families with joy.

Dear readers, have some compassion for your priest, rabbi or pastor. Make it easy for that person when he or she eulogizes you. We don't want to have to fudge our remarks about you. Leave us with some good material. Most clergy are happy to include a little hyperbole, but none of us enjoys bearing false witness about you when you are gone! And try your best to leave a legacy of good humor and joy. Try to leave your loved ones laughing through the tears in your memory. I hope you are living your lives in a way that brings this kind of pleasure to those who love you at the end! ✦

34

*I*t's in the Book

It should come as no surprise to you that I love the Bible. I would be an odd preacher if I didn't revere the scriptures. These sacred writings are a source of endless wisdom and insights upon which a person can build a good life. Open the Bible to any page, prick it and it will bleed with the force of life.

Now, I don't deny there are some spots in the Bible that will put the typical reader in a deep enough sleep to nap through a root canal. Take, for instance, the mind-numbing lists of "begats" in both the Old and New Testaments. Those begats are important, but unless you are an obsessive/compulsive genealogist, they may be a snoozer for you.

There are lots of fascinating things in the Bible. The Book of Esther in the Old Testament, for example, does not even mention the name of God. Nor does it focus on the towering spiritual themes of the Hebrew people. So it comes as no surprise that some rabbis disputed its inclusion in the Bible. In order to discover such unusual things about the Bible, one needs to read it!

I'm an enthusiast for many of the modern translations of the Bible. The most important thing is that we be able to read it with understanding. Of course, not many readers can read it in the original languages in which it was first written, so a good translation in modern English is a must for most of us. However, sometimes translators feel compelled to "clean up" the earthiness of the ancient text to ease its impact on modern sensibilities. So I love to read the classic King James Version of the scriptures. This translation is treasured for its poetic language, but it sometimes gives a modern reader a jolt with its more literal rendering of the ancient manuscripts.

My years of reading the Bible continue to bring unexpected surprises for me. Only last week I came across something I had not noticed before. I was reading 1st Samuel, chapters 5 and 6, in the King James Version, and suddenly the words "emerods in their secret parts" leaped off the page. I said "*Whoa!*" Yep, that's what we moderns call hemorrhoids. Some modern translations call them "tumors." That seems to me to be overly timid of modern translators. This mention of hemorrhoids was in reference to some plagues the Lord had sent upon the Philistine men. The Bible tells us the great and the small were smitten. Wow! That would be quite a woe!

Here's what caused the plagues of mice and hemorrhoids. These Philistines had defeated the Israelites and captured the Ark of the Covenant. Thirty thousand Israelite soldiers were killed. For seven months the Philistines kept the Ark, but things did not go well for them. When the plagues of mice and hemorrhoids fell upon them, they decided to send the Ark back to the Israelites. They also decided it would be a mistake to send it back empty. So they came up with a novel idea. They made five golden images or figures of mice and put them in the Ark. Then they added five golden images of hemorrhoids. They hoped this gesture would ease the Lord's anger toward them.

I confess that I can sort of visualize a statue of a golden hemorrhoid, but I leave that to your own imagination. Despite the candor of the King James translators, even *they* backed off their literal approach and spoke of "secret parts." *Whew!* You can decide for yourself to read the entire story. It's right there in The Book. Suffice to say, if you have a supply of Preparation H in your medicine chest, this biblical story will come alive with vivid, existential power for you! ✦

35

*T*he Storm Is Passing Over, Hallelujah!

One of my favorite verses in the Bible is John 11:35: "Jesus wept." One reason I love it is that it describes the scene when word came to Jesus that his friend Lazarus had died. He responded to the news with spontaneous emotion. It is what one expects from a true friend. Little vignettes like this make the Bible believable for me. They make it real and true to life.

Another reason I like the verse is that it is short… the shortest verse in the Bible. I'm living a long life and am glad for that. But I am coming to the conclusion that shorter is generally better than long in this world. I can remember the invention of the foot-long hotdog. It was a wonderful thing. I loved it because it was twice as long as the original. But the innovation of lengthening hotdogs never went any further than that. It's clear that to push that envelope would make the mustard and onions start falling off into your lap. Shorter in many things is better. If I could start over, I would make my sermons shorter for sure.

Another short verse in the Bible that is a favorite of mine: "It came to pass." This verse appears many times in the Bible, especially in the Hebrew Bible. It simply means, "It happened that…." But I have taken the liberty to think of it whenever something unfortunate, bad, uncomfortable or threatening arises. For instance, a storm arises and I console myself that it won't last forever with a philosophical shrug and "It came to pass."

This morning I turned on the news broadcast to get the latest news on the national and world economy crisis. My stomach churned as I then checked to see what effect the stock market crash has had on my pension fund. Not good. Then I thought of the anxiety and fears sweeping households everywhere.

I remembered the story of Jesus calming the storm on the Sea of Galilee: "He got up, rebuked the wind and said to the waves, 'Quiet! Be still!' Then the wind died down and it was completely calm." I turned on my favorite recording of Charles A. Tinley's 1905 song, *The Storm Is Passing Over, Hallelujah!* It is based on that Bible story. It restored my soul.

"O courage, my soul, and let us journey on,
For the night is dark, it won't be very long.
O thanks be to God, the morning light appears,
And the storm is passing over, Hallelujah!

"O billows rolling high, and thunder shakes the ground,
The lightening flash, and the tempest all around,
But Jesus walks the sea and calms the angry waves,
And the storm is passing over, Hallelujah!

"The stars have disappeared, and distant lights are dim,
My soul is filled with fears, the seas are breaking in.
I hear the Master cry, "Be not afraid, 'tis I,"
And the storm is passing over, Hallelujah!"

So if you are distressed and anxious, trembling with emotion, remember this: that's okay. Jesus wept. And as the Bible often says, "It came to pass." It won't rain always. As the great African-American hymn writer wrote with the memory of the bitter season of slavery still fresh, "The storm is passing over, Hallelujah!" This too shall pass. The important thing is to keep *Hallelujah* alive! ✦

36

*T*he Flood

I can't help it. I'm an early riser. One recent morning I woke up at 4:30 feeling great. I walked into the kitchen and found the mess I had left late the night before. I had watched parts of four basketball games and one football game while trashing the kitchen with late-night snacking. Instantly I knew I needed to make amends while my beloved still slept. So I loaded the dishwasher.

Now here is where my good intentions began to go wrong. We had just downsized our living space from a large house to an apartment for our senior years, and I had not yet used the new dishwasher. I noticed that the detergent bottle on the counter was smaller than I remembered. However, it didn't occur to me that this meant it was a very concentrated brand. So I did what you would expect: I administered a manly dollop into the detergent cup in the washer door, closed the door and started the machine.

Seconds later, soapsuds began pouring from the machine onto the kitchen floor! I made a joyful noise to the Lord and scrambled to find the mop! For the next two hours I fought the flow of foaming water. It was a titanic struggle. The tide rolled across the floor and threatened the dining room carpet. The cats ran terrified to the front door and cowered there while I mopped.

Soon I was so overheated and overwhelmed by the flow, I removed my shirt and used it to fight the flood. There I was, in nothing but my BVDs and clerical collar, trying to control a deluge of biblical proportion. It was not a pretty sight. But the battle was eventually over; victory was mine. I finally burst the countless bubbles (I never knew that bubbles could just sit in the sink forever unless you burst them individually).

A bit later my newly awakened darlin' stuck her head in to ask, "What happened in the kitchen?" So I confessed to her what I've just told you dear readers. She said to me, "Do you not know the difference between dish*washing* detergent and dish*washer* detergent? For the machine, you use the liquid in the big green bottle *under* the sink. The kitchen looks very nice, honey." She looked at me in my clerical collar and boxers "What would you like for breakfast?" We didn't discuss this again.

In my usual Southern-Fried spirituality mode, I'm now trying to identify some "learnings" from this experience. I learned it doesn't help in a domestic crisis to phone Martha Stewart for help. She doesn't mop. She's like your favorite television minister. Celebrities don't make house calls! This is why you need a real pastor, not just a good-looking image on a flat screen. If you don't have a pastor and you've got a crisis, call me! I'm not bad-looking and I do make house calls. Please confine your calls to me to spiritual matters. I have given up mopping until after next Lent and I don't do windows.

There I was, in nothing but my BVDs and clerical collar, trying to control a deluge of biblical proportion.

I learned that if you are going to create a calamity of some sort, try to make it one that smells good. There is no reason a stumble ought to create a stink. Our kitchen smelled like a citrus orchard for days. Ours smells swell! It's great. You might want to remember this technique as a follow-up the next time you bake a possum.

I also learned that one of the benefits to me in writing this blessed blurb is that I get to entertain myself for a little while each week. This is a big help because so much humor is off-color nowadays, and I'm easily embarrassed. The only thing that would make me happier is if I didn't have to force my sweetheart to read these ramblings. Sometimes I catch her in a weak moment, and she laughs anyhow. Then, so as not to encourage me in this, she says, "You are so full of...!" I love her colorful vocabulary! She used to be a Baptist, you know! ✦

37

A Cure for Unwanted Sales Calls

Judy is getting over her crankiness, but the past few months have been tough for her. I know this because I've known her well for a long, long time. I have observed her moods and I'm glad this recent spell is over. It all started when she began to approach her 65th birthday. That fact alone, I could tell, was slightly annoying for her. But then the telephone began ringing. The typical caller would begin, "Hello, Judy, how are you? How is the weather in North Carolina?"

Judy would reply with the weather report — snow in the higher elevations, rain along the coast, dry and sunny in the Piedmont with a cold front moving in from the north. Then the caller would say something like: "Well, Judy, you know you are going on Medicare soon. You are going to be 65 before long, hahaha! And you know Medicare is not going to provide sufficient coverage for your health care, teeheehee. You will need to have supplemental insurance so you won't be a burden on your children. How many grandchildren did you say you have?" By that time, Judy would catch on that the call was not from someone calling to remind her of the next book club meeting.

Well, the frequency of these calls rapidly increased over the next few weeks. She asked a friend in the insurance business to guide her and take care of this need. However, until her birthday, the calls just kept coming. They would start at eight a.m. and reach a crescendo at six p.m. after which they would taper off 'til bedtime. Her mood worsened over the weeks. Finally, the straw that broke the camel's back (so to speak) was when the caller was told that she had already taken care of the matter. He then asked her, "Would you be interested in a burial plot?"

My sunny disposition was transformed into something more like a winter squall.

You've got to admit, the woman deserves relief from this. Which brings me to the second part of this sermon about life! She finally, along the way, began to take the telephone off the hook for long periods of time. The house that had usually been filled with music playing in the background was now filled with the screech of the telephone, trying to get her to hang it up! The significant others in her life knew to call her on the cell phone — a number she carefully guarded. The whole atmosphere of the household became fouled and friends were troubled by the "busy" signal they always got when they tried to call.

Now, I tell you this tale of telephonic woe because I am confident many of you have been through the same ordeal. I myself languished in this condition last year. This was despite the fact that I had registered to be on the list to avoid "unwanted calls" for two years already. My sunny disposition was transformed into something more like a winter squall. I didn't like the way I began to think and feel. It became a matter of fairness and justice, kindness and civility for me. Now, I take my place on our journalistic street corner to say my piece.

Here is my solution: Let's require the telephone company, which charges us a fat but fair fee to have a phone in our homes for our own purposes, to deduct fifty cents from our bill and charge it back to any caller from a business number. They could do this. If you doubt it, take a look at the complexity of detail on your phone bill. This would be the right, fair and just thing to do. Be honest now: How many of you got your phone installed because you wanted to make it easier for unwanted business callers to wake you at eight a.m. on a Saturday morning or interrupt your evening meal? Of course, I know many people are trying to make a living working at these phone banks, but there's got to be a better way. I'm told they get paid very little too. However, somebody's making lots of dough from this.

Ah, well, if you need to reach me and find my number busy, send me an email. Or send a carrier pigeon. I wanted to give you my cell phone number, but my beloved told me I would be an idiot if I did that! ✦

38

The DMV and Mrs. Byrd's Painting

There's a quirky thing about me: I usually don't read my stuff. I just write it. I don't read it. I sure am glad y'all do though.

Now and then I hear from a reader who has found a typographical error in this divine stuff. In putting this book together, I read through many pieces I have written over the years and was shocked at how many errors I made. I'm glad to have had many fine editors who usually caught those flubs and prevented me frequent embarrassment.

Really, I never let a typo get me down. Sometimes I slip one in on purpose just to test reader alertness. I believe sometimes a typo stimulates a new thought. In fact, I'm reasonably relaxed about the little miscues in ordinary life.

Being cool and indifferent to little annoyances allows me to save up my steam and bluster to blow my top on big irritations. I'm talking about things that really matter, like getting a busy signal when making a telephone call. Or the annoying wait behind a fellow combing his hair and failing to move on when the traffic light changes to green. You know what I mean?

For instance, a recent six-hour wait in line at the Department of Motor Vehicles was a "losing my cool" kind of experience. The thought that kept running through my mind was: "Governor, if I were you, I believe I would take my picture off the wall here. That is, if I were ever interested in running for office again!" I think the DMV level of service ought to be the litmus test for incumbent state governments. Can you think of a better indication of an administration's competency and commitment to service?

I've always been pretty good at handling little glitches even in stressful situations. When I was a young guy courting Judy, I wanted to make a good impression on her mother. I was an art student at the time, and Judy asked and I agreed to paint a picture for her mother.

One afternoon I sat down in her yard and began painting a landscape. When I was almost finished, a bird flying over unceremoniously made a deposit on my masterpiece. Well, the paint was thick and wet and I couldn't wipe off that spot. I didn't want to start over and do an entirely new painting, so I just added a stem and some leaves to the bird dropping and made a flower of it.

My mother-in-law liked the painting. It hung in Mrs. Byrd's home 38 years until her death. I always thought of it as Mrs. Byrd's bird-flower painting. It was several years after I had married her daughter that I screwed up my nerve and explained that strange flower in the painting.

Mrs. Byrd's painting is at our house now. The bird blossom has long ago flaked off, but the stem and leaves are still there. There is also a faint shadow of the bird's contribution. As I look at it now, my painting is very amateurish, but the bird flower is masterful. The memory of how it was created is among my most precious treasures.

The moral of this story is that what a bird drops on your painting doesn't last, but the picture, if it is done for love, does. And the pleasure of the memory does too. Who knows? Maybe God sent that bird with the mission to remind me that the painting wasn't meant to be perfect. Only God is perfect. I don't know: it's just a thought. I do know this: typos always stir us up but ought never get us down. ✦

39

*M*avericks

I'm having trouble today writing this blessed blurb. The image on my computer monitor is quivering like a frightened bunny rabbit. Or maybe it is shaking with rage like a rattlesnake. I don't know which. Either way it's almost impossible to read what I'm writing. I think my monitor is simply about to give up the ghost. Or maybe it has decided to become a maverick.

That's a word a recent political season aroused for us when Senator McCain and Governor Palin claimed the "maverick" mantle for their presidential campaign. I went to the dictionary to refresh my mind on what a maverick is. *Maverick*: "A free range animal, especially a calf that has become separated from its mother, traditionally considered the property of the first person who brands it" (*The Free Dictionary*, online). Maverick is a term of endearment for many Americans. In the 1970s the Ford Motor Company first branded an auto a "Maverick," and it became their biggest seller ever.

Most of us Americans come from maverick stock, separated from our ancestral mother countries. I was reminded of this while attending my family reunion recently. We celebrated the memory of our family members who first came to America in 1738 from Germany. They were Lutherans looking for liberty in a new land. The first thing they did when they got settled near what is now Virginia Tech University was start a

Lutheran church. When the Revolutionary War broke out, they revealed their maverick-ism by enlisting in the Virginia Militia.

The other half of my ancestors came from England, and they displayed the same revolutionary inclinations. By the time of the Civil War, these families had migrated to East Tennessee and given up their maverick-ism. They had become intensely dedicated to the idea of the "United" States of America. They were fiercely devoted to freedom for all people and opposed to the idea of slavery. So they joined the Union Army — all except one old cousin, a free-range maverick, who became a Confederate, a rebel soldier. We don't know much detail about all of this except that family lore contains the following line about one old great-great-great-granddad: "He was captured, imprisoned and starved to death by Democrats (meaning Confederates) during the Civil War."

In every generation following the Revolutionary War era, our crowd has been a very un-mavericky bunch. We have struggled mightily to defend the "unitedness" of these States of America. Still, we treasure that maverick spirit of independence that marked our family at the beginning of our nation. We do this for mostly spiritual reasons.

We love the words in Galatians 5:1: "For freedom did Christ set us free: stand fast therefore, and be not entangled again in the yoke of bondage" (*American Standard Version*). This comment in its biblical context is, of course, a reference to spiritual bondage. However, we Americans have morphed it into a hybrid religious/secular/political truism. It's good for an election campaign to stimulate us to consider these things.

"For everything there is a season," reminds the writer of Ecclesiastes in the Bible. Today he might say, "There's a season for overturning and breaking, a season for rebuilding and renewing."

I wish this monitor screen of mine would quit trembling so I could see more clearly what I have written. It's important for us to know what we think — especially in an election season — lest we be like the wit who said: "Sometimes I don't know what I believe until I read it on a bumper sticker." ✦

40

*O*f Late Night Calls and Naked Dining

It seems like almost everybody is having trouble sleeping these nights. Lots of people are very restless in their sleep. My wife Judy was having trouble resting comfortably. She woke me up answering the telephone in her sleep. I heard her saying, "Hello. Hello." The trouble was, the telephone wasn't ringing. To make matters worse, apparently the person calling in her dream hung up on her.

She continued on in her sleep. However, by this time I was wide awake. I debated whether to tell her about her nocturnal activity. There is, after all, a kind of indignity about getting an imaginary phone call in the middle of the night and then being hung up on by the fictitious caller. The more I thought about it, the "awaker" I got. Eventually I got up, put on a pot of coffee and waited for sunrise. Then I went back to bed and slept soundly.

About 70 percent of folk claim they have trouble getting enough sleep. I figure this is partly because we Americans work too hard. People in other countries tend to work less and take more time off than we do. Instead of resting more, we tend to get a second job if we have some extra time.

This is one reason why it's important to go to church on Sunday mornings. It is a wonderful time to catch up on your sleep. We preachers are not judgmental about this. We even do what we can to encourage it. We pad the pews to make them more comfortable. Lots of churches allow about six feet of pew space per person so folk can lie down end-to-end if they wish. I'm waiting to hear that a new "Church of What's Happening Now" has installed reclining La-Z-Boy pews in their worship space.

We preachers do what we can to help. Back in the 1940s, the minister at First Methodist Church in Charlotte was Clovis Chappell, one of the most famous preachers in the world. Yet some of the "saints" had trouble staying awake. One hot summer Sunday — this was before air conditioning — Brother Chappell asked the ushers to open the stained-glass windows. He announced, "I can't bear to watch people sleeping in a poorly ventilated room."

Blessed are they who sleep during the sermon, for they are the ones with a clear conscience.

Once, when speaking to the Dilworth Rotary Club in Charlotte, I looked out into the crowd and noticed that a club member and beloved physician, the late Dr. Joe Van Hoy, was in the audience. Although I was just beginning, he was already relaxed, head bowed and with his eyes closed. I remarked that the sight of this made me feel at home because I saw this every Sunday morning at First Methodist Church, where I was minister.

I said, "Forgive me if I speak softly. I don't want to bother Dr. Joe." His posture didn't change and his eyes remained closed, but I heard his distinctive voice say, "Don't worry, Harold. You've never bothered me before!" If yours is a soft-spoken preacher, don't mistake this for a lack of conviction. Accept it as a mark of respect for those who are "resting in the Lord." Maybe the folk who sleep in the pews deserve a special beatitude: Blessed are they who sleep during the sermon, for they are the ones with a clear conscience.

I hope I can sleep better tonight than I did last night. I tossed and turned because of a nightmare. I dreamed I was dining in a restaurant. I discovered that, as the meal progressed, articles of clothing began to disappear from my body. Eventually, I was clad only in my necktie, shoes and socks. I was comforted by the napkin resting in my lap. Eventually I put the napkin over my face and walked out. I did not want anyone to recognize me! This is a troubling dream for me. One of you dear readers may want to explain it to me.

Through the years, I have often slipped into the church sanctuary when nobody else was there. I sat or knelt to pray for a while. I may do that again today — not to pray, but to stretch out on a padded pew to sleep. I'm still tired from last night! ✦

41

*W*riting About Chickens

Did you hear about the rare-book collector who met a man who said he had just thrown away an old Bible that had been packed away for several generations? "Somebody named Guten-something had printed it." "Not Gutenberg!" gasped the book lover "You have thrown away one of the most famous books ever printed. One copy recently sold for over four million dollars." The other man was unmoved. He said, "My copy wouldn't have been worth much. Somebody named Martin Luther had scribbled notes all over it."

I am a book lover and collector of books. Early in my ministry I was a publisher, editor, illustrator and writer of religious books. Inexperienced and ignorant in those days, I did not even think to keep a copy of everything I wrote and published. Now in these latter days, I wish I had been more thoughtful.

I don't even have a copy of each of these divine columns that I have written over the years. I wish I did. Maybe the Lord wishes I had lost a few more of these musings. I'm trying to be more careful and save them all now. I don't much care to re-read them, but I worry that I might repeat some of the yarns I have spun through the years. I have trouble remembering what I had for lunch yesterday. To remember what I wrote a few weeks ago is too much for me.

It took me years to develop a sense of the romance of books and writers. Today I can look at the autograph of an author written inside a book in my collection and be transported in my imagination into the personality of that person. The most treasured thing in my collection is a copy of *The Screwtape Letters,* signed by the author, C.S. Lewis. Ever since I first read this book many years ago, I have admired his ability to interpret the Christian faith. I have since read almost all his books.

> *I have helped countless chickens enter the ministry.*

Now, to look at the penciled signature of Lewis makes a great impact on my psyche and draws me close to him.

Another of my favorites was the great writer Rabbi Abraham Joshua Heschel. He had a great soul and knew about prayer. When asked, just before he died, what he had most wanted in life, he told a friend, "I asked for wonder." I look at his tiny, delicate signature, and I remember him and I want wonder too.

When I look over the things I have written during my 40-plus years of writing for publication, I am surprised by how little I've written about fried chicken. This is especially surprising because I have been a preacher so long. I have helped countless chickens enter the ministry. Also, many people, when remarking about this column, call it *The Southern-Fried Chicken*. It is understandable that folk misread *Southern-Fried Preacher* to be *Southern-Fried Chicken*. It's natural to associate a preacher with chicken. However, I haven't written much about Southern-fried chicken. Lots of other people smarter than I am have been silent on the topic too. However, if they *were* to respond in print to the question, "Why did the chicken cross the road?" here is what they might say...

Plato: "The chicken crossed the road for the greater good."

Aristotle: "It is the nature of chickens to cross roads."

Star Trek's Captain Kirk: "To boldly go where no chicken has gone before."

Karl Marx: "It was an historical inevitability."

In the interest of fair and balanced reporting, I asked a chicken why she crossed the road. She cackled, "You think that's funny, do you? Well, you just figure it out — smart guy!" ✦

42

Church of the Holy Oval

I am a racing fan. I should say I'm a NASCAR fan. I don't have much interest in the kind of racing they do up in Indianapolis. I think it's because I don't know the drivers in that kind of racing. But NASCAR, now that's a different kettle of fish. I think the NASCAR crowd is sorta like the population of a small Southern town. There's stuff going on all the time among NASCAR folk — arguments, rivalries, insults and fists. All these things are hurled amongst racers and fans but at the end of the day everybody still feels like part of one big family.

I haven't always been a racing fan. When I moved to Charlotte more than 20 years ago I became exposed to this phenomenon for the first time. I came to be the minister of the downtown First United Methodist Church. On the first big racing weekend after my arrival, my smart-alecky mouth got me in big trouble. From the pulpit that Sunday race day, I pondered the rhetorical question: Do race fans enjoy sitting by the cloverleaf over at the interstate highway watching the traffic whiz around? Well, you would have thought I had uttered a mild obscenity in the middle of the eleven o'clock service. I unwittingly ignited a firestorm of response.

I found in my sophisticated congregation a crowd of rabid race fans. They were professional people, highly-educated and dignified. They were old and young, male and female. Before the next big racing weekend I had numerous offers of free tickets to the races. A kind of evangelistic zeal broke out among some of my members trying to get me converted into a racing fan.

So I went to my first race that next October. Now I am a "born again" NASCAR fan. I was shocked at how little I really knew about racing and race fans. The first thing I learned is that fans come in all shapes and sizes. Almost as many fans are female as are male. That was a surprise to me. Also, not all fans are "Rednecks." Now, I use that word as a term of endearment. I myself am one — a Redneck I mean, and I love Rednecks. But I discovered that you don't have to be a Redneck to be a racing fan. All of my previous assumptions about racing turned out to be wrong.

I also discovered that racing is a very complex sport. Technology junkies (of which I am not one) can become immersed quickly in the intricacies of the machinery. It is also very hard to keep up with things happening on the track. Two cars can be running side by side at very high speeds but one can be two miles ahead of the other. It's hard to know who's ahead. Fortunately, a big sign keeps fans informed about who's leading and the order of those following.

You don't have to be a Redneck to be a racing fan.

One of the things I liked instantly about racing is that it is a great way to get away from all else competing for your attention. You can't hear your cell phone ringing. Nor can you carry on much of a conversation with your neighbor because of the noise. That can be a relief for anyone two or three times a year. Also, not too much changes over the course of 300 or 600 miles of racing. So you can get up and go to the restroom or get a hotdog. When you get back to your seat, they're still doing what they were doing when you left — riding around in circles. That's nice.

I discovered racing is a lot like church. It is loud and exciting at moments. Then there are long periods of monotony filled with wind and racket but going nowhere except toward the finish line. It isn't free. Tensions among attendees arise sometimes. Collisions can happen without warning. Lots of the experience is run under caution flags. The people are good at heart and are quick to respond when there is a heart-wrenching occurrence to someone in the family. And amidst all this, lots of folk get some badly needed sleep.

A fellow sitting beside me at the first race I attended fell over into my lap fast asleep on the final lap. He didn't even get to see the checkered flag and cheer the winner. He was out like a deacon at the end of the sermon. 'Course, over the several hours of the race, in the heat of the afternoon, he had put away four six-packs of cold Bud. He fought dehydration all day. It was a very hot day. I noticed that as the day wore on, he began to list over toward me. This was okay with me because I have often seen heads a-bobbing, leaning toward their neighbors on the pews while I was preaching. This was uncomfortable because it was so hot but I cut him some slack. However, I did object when he wet his pants. What's a neighborly fellow to do in a situation like this?

One of the things I liked instantly about racing is that it is a great way to get away from all else competing for your attention.

About an hour before the checkered flag fell, he fell completely over and rested his snoring head on my lap. I checked his pulse to make sure he was alive. Then as the stadium emptied out, I stretched him out on the bench with a "Now I lay him down to sleep" benediction and went home. That was my first racing experience.

Recently, my pal, the Reverend Merrill Perkins, his teenage grandson Austin and I attended the evening service at the Church of the Holy Oval. It is also known as the Lowes Motor Speedway. The occasion was the annual Coca-Cola 600 celebration. It had been about ten years since I had been to a race. My bad heart had been so bad I couldn't attend. Now, praise the Lord, I'm enough better to take my place in the pews once again.

Some things have changed since I was at a race in the past. For one thing, it costs a lot more to attend this church than it does to go to most churches. It cost $49 for an adult ticket. This was the cheapest ticket we could get. This may be because it was in the non-smoking, no-alcohol section.

Attendance is great at the Church of the Holy Oval. Most folk arrived an hour or two early even though we all had reserved seats. We were all so enthusiastic; we did not want to miss any of the excitement. Once I saw a sign posted in the stairwell of a church noted for its spirited services. The sign said: "No dancing on the stairs." I remember thinking, "I hope I live long enough to see a sign like that posted in a Methodist church." We never have to be worried that anyone will get bored at Holy Oval. Maybe we need to caution the saints at the Oval about the danger of shouting "Amen!" while jumping atop their pews. Someone might get hurt.

As it happened, we didn't get to have a race after all. I never even saw a race car. It turned out that the entire congregation was soaked in a mass baptism. The skies opened up and the rain fell upon the just and the unjust — to cite a verse from the Bible. After a three-hour rain delay, The High Priest from NASCAR pronounced the benediction with the announcement that they would try to run the race the next day at noon.

I didn't go back on Monday. I couldn't. I hated to have wasted $49 on a ticket. However, maybe the Lord thinks the Speedway owner needs the money more than I do. We are, after all, in this rough patch with the world economy. I've been blessed by having just enough so that losing $49 is not going to sink me financially. Still, that is probably the last race I'll attend. When rain is threatening, I think I'll probably skip church like lots of regular Christians do, and just stay home! ✦

43

$\mathcal{B}$lame It on the Ozone

Today is another code orange day for ozone in the atmosphere, and the temperature is headed once again for the century mark. That's my excuse, anyhow, for thinking sluggishly today. If you don't buy that one, I have several others I could offer.

Through the years, I have learned that, when I'm having a dull day, I can jumpstart my brain by making lists. The list can be about almost any topic. The mental exercise of making a list helps me get organized and focused. It helps me clarify ideas and even have a new thought or two.

So today I'm in my list-making mode. This list is comprised of some of the things I want most in life. I hope it will stimulate some of you, dear readers, to make your own lists. I think it is a good way to cultivate practical spirituality.

Here are my "Things I Want Most in Life":

(1) I want to be nothing that I am not.

(2) I want to have nothing that I cannot live without.

(3) I want to love people but possess no one and be possessed by no one.

(4) I want to help people know God well enough to love God.

(5) I want to understand God's expectations of me.

(6) I want to have enough nerve to live up to God's expectations of me.

(7) I want to help people live out of their larger rather than their lesser selves.

(8) I want to exhort, encourage, cajole, aggravate and tease society into deeper compassion, truer justice, greater liberty and genuine peace.

(9) I want to have a sense of humor that prevents me taking myself too seriously.

(10) I want an attitude of gratitude that helps short-circuit my natural inclination to self-absorption.

That's my list for today. Ten items on a list are plenty. If Moses had larger stone tablets on Mt. Sinai, he might have brought down 11 commandments. The eleventh commandment might have been: "Thou shalt not have more than ten commandments. Ten are enough. Y'all (Moses was a Southern-Fried Preacher.) are going to have your hands full obeying these ten."

However, since I'm not Moses, and I'm not sitting on top of a mountain chiseling in stone, I think I'll add another item to the list of things I want most in life. Number 11: I want always to be risking something for God's sake. The key words here are "for God's sake."

Moses was a Southern-Fried Preacher.

One of the problems in many churches is the reluctance to risk much for God's sake. That's why, on the railroad of life, we religious folk are so often found crammed into the caboose — bringing up the rear. I want to be up near the engineer so I can see what's ahead and where I'm going. That's just the way I am. It takes a bit of risk to get the most out of life!

Speaking of risk and reward, did you hear about the freshman at the university who was about to go out on her first blind date? Her roommate, who was making the arrangements, asked whether she preferred Southern guys or Northern guys. The freshman was from a small Midwestern town and innocently unaware of distinctions between the two. She asked, "What's the difference?"

Her worldly-wise roommate replied, "Southern guys are more romantic. They will take you walking in the moonlight, whisper sweet nothings in your ear and kiss you on the veranda. Northern guys are more active. They like to take you to exciting places and do exciting things."

The young woman pondered the differences and then asked wistfully, "Could you please find me a Southern guy from as far north as possible? And, by the way — what's a veranda?"

That's the other thing about these blazing-hot days when the air quality has gone bad. The corniest old jokes emerge from the dust of the past — seeking fresh air, I suppose. I'm blaming all of this on the ozone. ✦

44

A Graduation Speech

We are about to enter the season of school graduations for this year. I always enjoy this season.

As usual, there are a few controversies regarding commencement speakers. Recently the choice of having President Obama as a speaker stirred up a couple of hornet's nests. The cause of these dust-ups usually has something to do with religion or politics. Well, folk have a right to feel strongly about their religion and their politics. I won't deny that. I once spoke at a high school ceremony as a substitute for the minister who had been invited by the school principal. That minister had made some public statements that had so outraged the senior class, they threatened to boycott the event if he were to be the speaker. So the principal then asked me if I would do it. I was happy to oblige.

I'm not speaking at any such events this year, but I've been thinking about what I'd say if I were. Naturally, a major part of a commencement speech is to challenge the graduates in their pursuit of a great life. Since I am an enthusiast for such a theme and have had such a great life myself, I'd jump right into that topic.

The first thing I'd tell them is to *cultivate their imaginations*. I'd share something Michelangelo once said to explain his sculpting approach: "I saw an angel in the marble and I carved until I set him free." How would the world be different if more of us could imagine the angels in the stones?

Then I'd talk to the graduates about *illuminating their dreams.* Too often our dreams are burned off by that first cup of coffee in the morning and never make it into anything real and beautiful. By nightfall those dreams are lost even to our own memories. Schools ought to be graded on how well they teach their students to dream. I'd tell my graduates what Vincent van Gogh said: "I dream my painting and then I paint my dream." To be able to dream beautiful dreams and then make those dreams visible to others — now *that* makes for great contributions to humanity.

Of course, a speech to graduates needs to include a *summons to risk-taking.* A life that always plays safe, usually — all too soon — plays out. Oh, I don't mean it ends. I mean it just settles into boredom. I'd tell the new grads what Martin Luther King Jr. said: "Faith is taking the first step even when you don't see the whole staircase." Karl Barth, a great 20th-century theologian, told about the man climbing a long, dark stone staircase in a medieval tower. As he groped his way upward, he suddenly lost his footing and began to fall. He blindly flailed his arms and, in the darkness, grabbed a rope — and rang the bell!

The last point I'd make in my speech is that a great life requires that at least some, if not all, of the *things we do must be done for love.* Make your spirituality driven by love more than duty, obligation or fear. Make a family for love. I'd remind the graduates of this bit of wisdom by Confucius: "Choose a job you love and you'll never have to work a day in your life." That's the truth. If the great philosopher had not beat me to it by 2,500 years, I would have said that myself.

Finally, I'd tell them that if they follow this path, they will have great, long lives. The late, great comedian George Burns observed, as he enjoyed his wonderful life of 100 years: "First, you forget names, and then you forget faces. Next, you forget to pull your zipper up and finally you forget to pull it down!"

I say, that's the truth! And that's all right! If you do these things, you will leave yours a better and happier world for your having been here! ✦

45

Ah, for a Childlike Faith

She was a tiny little girl, just three years old, but spiritually precocious and talkative. Sitting in the bathtub one night, she asked her mother a question. Her mother called in the father, saying to her daughter, "Honey, ask your Daddy that question."

The little girl looked up at her father and with a dramatic shrug said, "Well, I was just sitting here in the bathtub having beautiful thoughts about life and love and things like that and I wondered, is that God talking to me?"

The father said, "Wow, sweetie, maybe so. Isn't that wonderful?" She replied, "Well, no. Actually, it is beginning to get on my nerves."

Later that week the child asked her mother, "Mommy, does God see everything we do?" Her mother replied that God not only *sees* everything we do, God *hears* everything we say and even *knows* everything we think. To which the little one observed, "Now that's sneaky, isn't it?"

That incident happened at our house and the little girl was our daughter, Susannah. She is a young adult now and soon to receive her Master's degree from Emory University's School of Theology.

When I read the comments of Jesus about how we must all come to the Kingdom of Heaven as little children, I think of this little girl and so many, many similar instances of childlike spirituality. This is what marks the difference between child-*ish*-ness and child-*like*-ness — the ability to look with wonder and awe. A child is intently eager to know and grow. Add to that the child's ability to trust and believe.

Most folk quickly surrender their child-*like*-ness to child-*ish*-ness as they grow older. We become more cynical and less able to trust. We become more self-serving and less able to think of the needs of others.

It is very hard for most of us adults to believe, truly believe, like a child can believe. We affirm our faith often in a liturgical sense. But when it comes to actually believing in our hearts what we say with our lips, it gets very difficult indeed. Why do I say this? I say it because if we truly believed as a child can believe — that God is here and knows everything we say, think and do — would we not live our lives somewhat differently?

It is very hard for most of us adults to believe, truly believe, like a child can believe.

Jesus says it is as hard for a rich man to enter the Kingdom as it is for a camel to get through the eye of a needle. It may also be as hard for an adult to get into the Kingdom as it is for an elephant to get through a child's playhouse door. It isn't impossible. It's just very hard.

So what can we do about it? One thing we can do is *rediscover playfulness*. We can laugh more. We can delight in others and think less of ourselves. We can embrace a gentler, kinder view of God. We can blame God less and thank God more. We can sing more and immerse ourselves in beauty. We can give more without expecting anything in return. We can break out of our habits of cynicism and complaint. We can simply live out of our larger and not our lesser selves.

It doesn't take long for a child to experience an erosion of the childlikeness that is a passport to the Kingdom. Soon the child begins to mimic the childishness of adulthood. Then the challenge becomes much harder — the rediscovery of childlikeness.

When I was a young preacher, I was asked by a man in his early seventies for an odd pastoral service — to administer infant baptism to him. He was a man of many problems. He was addicted to prescription drugs and had multiple health problems. He had never been baptized, although he was a man of considerable religious faith. But he had observed the rite of infant baptism many times. He had noted the promises of the parents and the congregation to nurture and rear the child in the knowledge of God, until such time as the child would embrace Christ as his or her personal Savior. He wanted that kind of nurture for himself. I thought then and now, many years later, that here was a man nearing the Kingdom as he recognized his child-like need for God. A few weeks later, he met God face-to-face. ✦

Our Susannah, all grown up

46

$\mathcal{I}$ Bought Myself a Speedo

This gnarled old preacher has learned that one surefire way to perk up his reader ratings is to write about animals: cats, dogs and such. I have resorted to that ploy many times through the years and have often written about wildlife. I've rhapsodized about birds, squirrels, possums, armadillos, whales, elephants, Baptists, etc. I'll write about almost anything to try to wake up a crowd.

Recently I was telling the staff of this dignified newspaper about losing my swimming trunks at the beginning of last summer. I went over to the mall and bought me a Speedo. Now, some of you more pious folk will claim not to know what a Speedo is and will have to consult your grandchildren. Suffice to say, it is a scanty type of bathing garment, but it is also a well-known brand name in swimwear. As you would expect, I bought a rather conservatively cut Speedo. I can't swim. I mostly just pose. I have found that I can swiftly empty a swimming pool simply by showing up! The people at the newspaper are scared half to death about what I might write when hot summer swimming weather returns. (This is my clever way to teach them to pray.)

But back to my topic for today. I've written lots about animals. This always works to attract readers. However, there is a second way to draw a crowd, and that is to write about puns.

Everyone loves puns. Oh, I know we all groan and moan at punsters. However, we secretly love puns because we know you have to possess strong language skills to understand puns. Punsters are far more intelligent than non-punsters, and the punsters know this. So if you don't like puns, we punsters understand, and you can quit reading now. We love you and will see you back here soon with a different topic.

Now, for all of you bright folk, the rest of this divine drollery is going to be punny. Not too long ago, Cousin Jim's wife, Melanie Harless, from Oak Ridge, Tennessee, sent me a bunch of puns. I'll start with some secular ones and end with some that have more or less religious connotations.

(1) Two hydrogen atoms meet. One says, "I've lost my electron." The other asks, "Are you sure?" The first replies, "Yes, I'm positive." (Now, you would expect a pun like that from someone living in the Atomic City.)

(2) A vulture boards an airplane carrying two dead raccoons. The flight attendant says, "Sorry, sir, only one carrion per passenger." (The rules are changing these days for air travelers.)

I can't swim. I mostly just pose.

(3) The Buddhist refused Novocain during a root canal. His goal was to transcend dental medication. (Ouch, that one hurts!)

(4) A group of friars were behind on their belfry payments, so they opened a small flower shop to raise funds to help out. While some people thought it a good idea to buy flowers from the men of God, the rival florist who had a shop across the street felt it was unfair competition. He requested that the friars close the shop, but they refused. He begged them to close. Still they refused. In desperation, he hired the toughest thug in town, Hugh MacTaggart, to "persuade" the friars to close down

their shop. He beat the friars up and trashed their shop. Terrified, they went out of business. Which proves that only Hugh can prevent florist friars.

Okay, okay, I admit that some puns are punnier than others. You are entitled to your own personal reactions. Which reminds me of the fish that swam into a concrete wall and said, "Dam." By the way, don't you wish we had some pleasant, more genteel oaths for such things as this these days? ✦

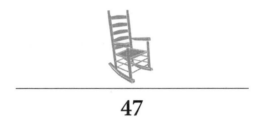

47

*G*od Bless the Doctors

I was doing a little weekend household project requiring the use of a razor-sharp utility knife. I was careless and let the knife slip, slicing through the fat part of my palm where the thumb connects. Well, with blood squirting and wife Judy getting more frantic by the second, we went to a nearby Urgent Care clinic. While the doctor was stitching up my hand, he tried to give me a little encouragement. He said, "Actually, this is your lucky day. This is *Free Rectal Exam Week* here at the clinic."

When he felt me tense up, he tried to redeem the situation by saying, mostly for the overbearing and worried wife sitting anxiously by, "Now, you are not to lift anything heavier than a beer or the television remote control. You could still lose this hand, ya know!"

Although I'm not a drinker, he won my heart with that remark, since I am a compulsive user of the TV clicker. I said to him, "You're the kind of doctor I believe I can put my confidence in."

Early in life I had a doctor whose stock advice was, "Take two aspirin and send a check in the morning." Then I had one who usually said, "Lose some weight — that'll be $65, please." After that, I had a series of doctors who have been not only great doctors but also great friends. Because I have several serious health problems, I have several doctors to whom I have immense gratitude.

On top of that, I have been the pastor to lots of fine physicians who have become wonderful friends to me. It is reassuring to see them in church on Sunday mornings. John Tuttle and Dennis Caudill are current examples. They are like younger brothers to me. They are bound to be losing money on me. They spend loads of time answering my questions. I am a test for their medical imaginations. This is a marvelous thing for me. They, along with my wife Judy, are keeping me alive. Judy is sometimes asked how it is that, despite my tremendous heart problems, I am still alive. She usually replies, "God has more things for him to do." Sometimes she adds, "And so do I!"

Many years ago, we had a next-door neighbor who was a professor at Vanderbilt University School of Medicine in Nashville. One day he brought home some old stethoscopes and gave them to the children in the neighborhood. Our son Philip was five years old at the time. He went around the house checking every beating heart — ours, the dog's, his own. He thought it was great. He was aware that I had recently received my doctor's degree from Vanderbilt, so one day he listened to my heart and asked, "Dad, why aren't you like Dr. Hollifield? The kind of doctor who helps people?"

Of course, I know Him who is the Great Physician. That ultimately explains everything. ✦

48

Preaching Myself to Sleep

Last Sunday I achieved something I always thought I was capable of doing: finally, I preached myself to sleep.

Not only that, I also fell backwards out of the pulpit. It was a three-foot fall from our traditional elevated pulpit. I landed on my head and back, with my feet still up on the floor of the pulpit — basically upside down. It was agreed that divine Providence must have guided my landing. As I fell, I avoided striking lots of hard corners and angles in the close quarters of the space … and I didn't damage the nearby organ. I'm told I made a resounding thud when I hit the floor. To those listening out in the congregation, I just disappeared from view.

Through the years I have put many listeners to sleep with my orations. However, this was a first for me. I knew something was amiss when I stood to climb into the pulpit to preach. I suddenly became drenched with perspiration, and by the time I opened the Bible, my vision had become blurred. I could not read my scripture, so I winged it and recited it from memory. Then as I started my message, I realized I was really in trouble. I was dizzy, but I could hear my voice, and I seemed to be staying on my message. As I continued, I was aware that the faces of my congregation were growing fuzzy. Also, in my own ears, my voice was becoming fainter.

While I continued to speak, I had a consultation with myself in my mind. Do I confess to the congregation that I am experiencing some difficulty and sit down? Or do I plunge ahead and hope this strange feeling passes? I did the latter. It did not pass. So I held onto the sides of the pulpit and forged ahead into the fog. Eventually, I remember hearing myself say "amen."

The next thing I saw was the face of a physician from the congregation peering into my face while checking my pulse. Other familiar faces were looking down at me. I have a vague memory of hearing someone say, "Call 911." I also have a vague memory of hearing my own voice. Witnesses tell me that I asked one of my ministerial colleagues to take a collection, lead a hymn and close the service. I also said, "Please ask folk to be generous with their offering!" I'm told that I asked of those who had come to my assistance, "Do any of you have a sermon in your pocket that you can give at the next service?"

Lots of people tell me it was a pretty good sermon. I don't know about that — I was on autopilot at the time. I'm glad to report that I must not have totally dozed off. While I don't remember the fall, apparently even in my semi-conscious state, my brain and mouth kept working. If I had gone on to glory at that moment, I would have liked for my epitaph to read: "As he left, he took a collection. He was a loyal preacher to the end."

Witnesses tell me that I asked one of my ministerial colleagues to take a collection, lead a hymn and close the service.

It turns out this entire stir happened, apparently, because of a surge in my blood sugar, a drop in my blood pressure and a "cardiac event" — all as I stood and climbed into the pulpit. I stayed three days in the hospital and am still getting things regulated. Because I had five bypasses six months ago, I underwent lots of heart tests while hospitalized. All seems okay in that regard.

However, as this column goes to press, I will be receiving the installation of a combination defibrillator and pacemaker. This will be a big help if my heart ever decides to act up in the future. I will also be participating in a research project with this new contraption for up to three years. My wife, Judy, is not excited about me being part of a research study. I think she fears I will turn into a 200-pound guinea pig. Having a research rodent as a mate is not what she had in mind when she married me over 43 years ago. A Baptist at the time, Judy could accept a Methodist like me, but a laboratory rat for a husband may be pushing the envelope a bit.

At the moment, I'm trying to think of what I can do for an encore next Sunday. Maybe I'll do a swan dive off the front of the pulpit and see if I can reach the third row of pews when I land. I'll do most anything to wake up a crowd. ✦

49

$\mathscr{A}$ Sermon: The Patriots

Delivered on a Sunday, July 3

It is for freedom that Christ has set us free. Stand firm, then, and do not let yourselves be burdened again by a yoke of slavery. (Galatians 5:1 NIV)

I love this time of year. It's a kind of patriotic sandwich of a season. Less than a month ago we celebrated Memorial Day. Then we remembered D-Day. Tomorrow we will celebrate Independence Day. We owe it to our forefathers and foremothers to know about these benchmarks of our national history. We owe it to our children and grandchildren to teach them the pathways in which they need to walk, lest they fail to receive full benefit in their future. Oh, my friends, we need to learn history! We owe it to God to learn who we Americans are, how we got here and where God wants us to be going. We owe it to God!

It once could be assumed that every school child could be expected to know the fundamentals of American history. Now even people who aspire to and serve in national office cannot be assumed to know even the basic story of our national history. God wants us to know something! If you are foggy on some aspect of history, ask my friend Max Chandler — he's a historian! Or ask me — I stayed awake in history class! Or read a book. Or watch the History Channel. In public life today everyone has an *opinion*. God wants us to *know* something!

I just wanted to come today to remind you what the Word of God says about **freedom**! "It is for freedom that Christ has set us free. Stand firm, then, and do not let yourselves be burdened again by a yoke of slavery."

I think the reason I get so soggy around the gizzard at times like this is that I have had to celebrate these days alone while in other countries several times. There's nothing quite like the sight of an American flag flapping gently in the breeze outside an American consulate in some foreign land when I am in a patriotic frame of mind. Especially when the minds of those around me are on other things. It invariably causes me to want to stand on a stump alongside a busy street and shout: "Friends, I'd like to say a few good words about America!" I have enough sense to refrain from such a thing. Instead, I just try to do what you do in such a circumstance; I try to be the best American abroad I can be.

This is a time for pulling together in the America we love.

Of all the places in the world where my patriotic emotions overflow, the Normandy American Cemetery on the bluff above Omaha Beach is the most powerful for me. An easy drive from the port city of Bayeux, France, the cemetery seems suddenly to appear from among the small villages dotting the countryside. Nothing can quite prepare a visitor for the exquisitely manicured site.

Memorial marble stands silent witness to the hallowed ground. The stunning dignity of the 9,387 white Vermont marble crosses aligned with amazing precision cause your breath to catch in your throat. It is an open-air sanctuary where visitors stroll, oblivious to time, reading names and dates of those whose bodies lie buried there.

Peering down on the beach from the heights, now quiet except for the gentle tides, one contemplates the heights of heroism the patriots attained on June 6, 1944, and the days following. It stirs in me the kind of emotions for America that I feel for my dearest family and friends. I only know to call it love.

There is poetry in such moments. I remember these words of John F. Kennedy: "When power leads man toward arrogance, poetry reminds him of his limitations. When power narrows the area of man's concern, poetry reminds him of the richness and diversity of existence. When power corrupts, poetry cleanses." That's what I hope for in this patriotic season: a cleansing, poetic meditation on what in us is true, just, noble and pure. Walt Whitman said, "The proof of a poet is that his country absorbs him as affectionately as he has absorbed it." I hope for less bombast and more poetry in our national discourse. Give me a lot less political gamesmanship and a lot more common cause in this time.

This is a time for pulling together in the America we love. One of the saddest things an American leader ever said was by Herbert Hoover: "I'm the only person of distinction who has ever had a Depression named for him." I hope and pray that a year from now we will have achieved a level of national unity and maturity that will engulf our national leaders in such honor and gratitude that no comment so sad will cross the minds of our people any more.

I'm back now at the Normandy American Cemetery for one last look. I see two crosses, side by side: a father and son. There are 33 pairs of brothers there. General Colin Powell once said: "Over the years, the United States has sent many of its fine young men and women into great peril to fight for freedom beyond our borders. The only amount of land we have ever asked for in return is enough to bury those that did not return." As we stand to sing now, let us, under God, salute that flag with hands on our hearts or with our hands to our foreheads. When we are at our best, God blesses America. Now let us salute America and bless God for her! Amen. ✦

50

*R*emembering

I am not the oldest person you know, but I am old enough to enjoy remembering. I'm also getting better at it. There was a time when I was neither very good at recalling nor in the least interested in it. Times change.

I began my ministry as pastor of two small Methodist churches near Athens, Tennessee. Judy and I had two babies at the time and had taken a 95 percent reduction in family income upon entering the ministry. It was 1965, and my salary was $100 per month. I mention that only to establish the setting for my story.

When we arrived, we discovered that neither church had a piano player. The truth was, the singing was awful. Spirited, but awful — a joyful noise. Even at the very beginning of my ministry, I had enough sense to recognize that music is at the heart of worship. I knew we had to do something to improve the music. So Judy and I invested $25 — a whole week's salary — in five piano lessons for her so she could help us sing better at those churches. She learned to play about a dozen songs in the hymnal. If we hadn't been so poor, she could have learned more songs.

Eventually, whenever we walked through the doors of those churches, the hymnals would flop open to one of those songs. I was the preacher and song leader; Judy was the piano player. We stayed there two years, and the only songs we sang were those few. Then the bishop moved us on to a larger responsibility.

Since we moved from there, nobody has asked her to play the piano nor me to sing. Now, I assure you, I'm not fishing for any invitations. Neither she nor I would, under any circumstances, ever try that again. The plain truth is that I never could stand to hear her play, and she refuses to listen to me sing.

Gasoline was cheap, of course, in 1965, but I couldn't afford much. I usually bought a dollar's worth at a time. I once ran out of gas while driving in a funeral procession. Fortunately, I managed to coast to a stop at the gravesite. After the burial, I was too embarrassed to admit this to anyone, so I walked home, got a gas can, bought 50 cents worth of gas and walked back.

Those days have marked me in some ways that linger on. For example, I frequently top off my gas tank. I never let the level get below a quarter of a tank. The way fuel prices are climbing nowadays, I may resort to buying a gallon at a time again. Also, I seldom go to the grocery without coming home with some toilet tissue. Fortunately, I can't remember any specific incident that relates to that.

I owned only one suit back in those days and wore it only on Sundays. I left it at the dry cleaners one week. When I went to pick it up on Saturday afternoon, unbeknownst to me, I was given another man's freshly cleaned suit. I discovered this the next morning when I dressed to go to church. That Sunday morning I preached in jeans and the only white shirt I owned.

If we hadn't been so poor she could have learned more songs.

I know about the Great Depression only from books and memories of others. However, when tough economic times come, I have enough memories of my own to know how stressful it can be.

This is such a time for many families in our country. I wish I had more confidence that someone somewhere, like in Washington, D. C., actually knows what to do about our stumbling economy and the loss of jobs. There is a certain logic to the theory that a big tax cut for the wealthy will inject more money into the creation of more jobs. It seems to me that tax cuts should be for people who live from paycheck to paycheck and who spend every penny they have only to get by. They would put all their money into buying the products and services the workers produce. Businesses would need to grow to meet the demand. Jobs would be created and wealthy people would benefit too.

But what do I know? I just worry about folk who worry about getting through the month. ✦

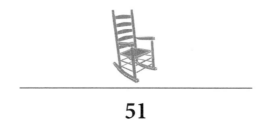

51

$\mathcal{I}$ Had a Curse Put on Me

I answered the telephone and got the fabulous news that I had won the New York lottery sweepstakes on June 6. "Over $2,000,000," the caller said. My reply was that this was not possible, because I had never entered the New York lottery or any other sweepstakes. The caller insisted that this was a special, promotional lottery somehow selected from zip codes or area codes or something like that. He began to give me rather elaborate directions about how to verify my winnings and arrange delivery by mail or wire. I won't recount the details but I thought, "There's some potential here for benefiting the readers of this pricelessly cheap column."

Here's how my thinking went: I'm a Methodist preacher, and my church has historically opposed gambling. Part of the argument rests on the idea that folk ought to work for what they have. Also, the poor tend to suffer most from the downside of gambling. *But …* I thought if I should ever get a boatload of money, I could give it away to people who need it. Oh, I'd pay off a few bills and give a wad to the church and some charities, but most of it I would give to you, dear readers. I'd devise some scheme to make sure it would only go to folk who actually read this divine drollery. I wouldn't want any of it to go to people who are too snooty to read this blessed blurb.

It would be wonderful fun to give away all that loot! I'd have a clear conscience for winning all that swag and make all my friends happy too. I'd rescue my reputation also, because I have never given any of you birthday gifts or Christmas presents. I'm a pretty generous fellow, but you wouldn't know it if I didn't tell you. So I listened to the caller.

At about halfway through the call, the Mother Superior of our household came into the room and began overhearing the call. She figured out what it was about and whispered, "How much?" I put my hand over the telephone and whispered that it was millions. She said, "I'd like to buy a shaggy rug to put in front of the bathtub." I nodded approval. I put my forefinger to my puckered lips so she would lower her voice and enable me to hear the caller's instructions. He was talking about a $102 administrative fee to get the loot to me.

I thought if I should ever get a boatload of money I could give it away to people who need it.

Well, to make a long story short, eventually I told the caller that I was not interested in pursuing my winnings. I only had $100 at the time and I needed to buy a gallon of gas.

He asked, "What should we do with your winnings?" I replied that he could do whatever he wished with them. At that point he said something, which I will not repeat here, and that I should "go to hell." Then he hung up. I did too.

Over the next few minutes the phone rang a few times but nobody said anything when I answered. Then I went online and filed a complaint with the Federal Communications Commission about fraudulent and harassing telephone calls.

But all is not lost! Just now, while I was writing this tale of woe, the mail arrived. In it was a notice from my retirement pension board. It was to inform me that my account had been reviewed and it was discovered that I did not receive a cost of living increase at the beginning of the year. I have been shorted $1.66 per month! So, even though I won't be able to divvy up more than $2,000,000 in lottery winnings to y'all readers, I'll be glad to share my $1.66 with you. At least you know my heart is in the right place!

The rest of the good news is that the curse the fellow put on me frightens me not one bit. I have good reason to expect that *his* eternal destination will be the final curse he tried to put on me! ✦

52

$\mathcal{S}$erendipity

I am sure most of you dear readers know the word serendipity. It is usually defined as when someone finds something good that they didn't expect to find. Or it is sometimes called a happy accident. Well, friends (and I do mean friends!), I have had a serendipitous past few days.

You remember, don't you, that I wrote about getting a phone call from a generous fellow telling me I had won millions of dollars in the New York lottery? *(See: I Had a Curse Put on Me)* And I told you about how, thanks to my well-honed, sharp-as-a-tack-mind, I saw right through his clever scam.

The mail then arrived containing a letter telling me I had been shorted $1.66 per month since January in my pension check. In my joy at this announcement, I impulsively promised —possibly with too much exuberance—to share my new largesse with you, my faithful friends and readers. And I fully intend to do that. I have now begun attempting to figure out how to administer the distribution of this bonanza. I'm finding this more of a challenge than I expected.

In the first place, I wanted to benefit as many people as possible. I also reasoned that it would only be fair for me to withhold any expenses I might incur in making the distribution. I decided I would need to mail the proceeds to you fortunate recipients by first-class mail. Parcel post, I concluded, would be less dignified and slower, and I ruled that out as the ideal method of delivery.

My next challenge came when I deducted 43 cents for each first-class stamp. Doing so made me able to buy three stamps but left only 37 cents to distribute to the recipients. This meant I could give 12-1/3 of a cent to each of three recipients. Well, you can see how silly it would be to try to saw a penny into three pieces.

In many things we preachers see mini-sermons. In this case it is a parable about the difficulty of meting out justice and fairness. However, not to be deterred from my goal, here is how I solved the dilemma.

First, I wrote a check for $1.66. Then I cut the check into thirds and put 1/3 in each of the three envelopes and sealed them. Then I grappled with the biggest serendipity of all.

My column had generated a mountain of letters and emails from you faithful friends. I got more mail in response to the epistle I wrote making this promise than to any other column I have ever written. They almost all begin, "Dear My Best Friend Harold, I read where you are going to share your newfound monthly boon of $1.66 from your pension with us!"

I told you about how, thanks to my well-honed, sharp-as-a-tack-mind, I saw right through his clever scam.

Then the writer usually says something like, "You know how I love the stuff you put in the paper. I am even home-schooling my shiftless husband using your column as my curriculum. I have him up to the third grade now!" Then some added something like, "All of us at the place where we get our nails done think you are the cutest thing alive and you are all we talk about…."

Well, folks, it goes on and on. So now I have to figure out to whom I send these 12-1/3 cent shares each month. This means in a year I'll have to send out 36 of these things. On top of that there is this question: What bank is going to cash 1/3 of a check for 12-1/3 cents? This will make your hair hurt!

So here is what I *finally* decided to do. I am going to present $1.66 in cold cash to one person each month. How will I decide who gets the loot? It must go to someone who reads and ponders this propitious pamphlet each week. And, most important, it will go to the first person each month that treats me to breakfast at the Waffle House.

Happy serendipity! ✦

53

*O*ur 50ᵗʰ Anniversary

On December 18, 2009, my beloved and I observed our 50th anniversary. This is a pretty big deal, so we had been thinking about how to celebrate it. Many people go somewhere exotic for these special occasions. One night Judy asked me what I would like to do. I suggested we go bungee jumping. This, you know, involves attaching an elastic cord to yourself and jumping off a tall structure of some sort. Just before you hit the ground, the cord snaps you back from splattering and you just dangle there.

I remember seeing news reports a few years ago about a man doing this on his 100th birthday. He plunged more than 200 feet. There was a picture of him in the newspaper. He looked a lot like the farmer with the pitchfork in the famous painting *American Gothic*, except he was wearing an old leather World War I aviator's cap. There he stood with a rather stoic look on his face with the earflaps of his cap curled up on the sides of his head. Beneath the picture was the caption that explained: "He felt a little ill after the jump, asked for his teeth back, went home and took a nap!"

My princess didn't respond immediately to my bungee-jumping suggestion, so I tried again: "We could go rafting down the Nantahala Gorge over in the mountains. The river, which is icy cold in the middle of August, would be truly arctic in mid-December. We could set the *Guinness* world record for goose bumps." I reminded her of what fun we had when we were younger and took the grandchildren on such an excursion. That was about 20 years ago and, surely, 20 years can't have made all that much difference in our physical condition. She listened patiently and finally said: "Please put your shirt on and quit being disgusting."

Then we began to chat about how content we are at this point in our lives. We have gone through the process of simplifying our lives. We divested ourselves of 50 years of accumulated stuff and moved into a cozy apartment. We don't buy much anymore. We spend lots more time at home, and we laugh a lot. Finally Judy said: "I would like to have a little gold chain. And I would like to go out for a nice steak dinner. I can't cook steaks very well anymore." More than 50 years ago, Judy was the *National Jr. Cook of the Year*. She's still the best cook I know! A simple celebration sounded terrific to me.

Coincidentally, yesterday I was looking through a pile of clippings and notes that I have tossed into a box through the years. Who knows why they caught my attention and caused me to save them? My strong, neat penmanship suggests I was much younger when I wrote one little page with two items on it. The first was a comment by a wife about her husband: "When I first met him, I noticed he was outstanding in his field … in the rain."

The second bit was the following: "A wife shot her husband at short range. The homicide investigator asked the first officer on the scene, 'Any residue of powder on the body?' The officer replied, 'Yes, sir. That's why she shot him!'"

Here is my theory to explain why I kept these old notes. In the first case, I have often been found out standing in the rain. The second story may explain why my sweetheart has never shot me! ✦

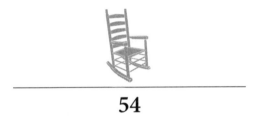

54

The Fine Art of Sweetheart-ery

I love to celebrate St. Valentine's Day, and each year I try to stir up among my dear readers a little electricity about real love. This is not an era in which it is easy to focus on *sweetheart-ery* — real romance. The air is filled with sound and fury about sex. We once described sex as the act of "making love." We no longer even attempt to make that connection any more. Most of our public conversation these days is coarse discourse about everything else but real love.

I don't know much to say about sex. I have led such a sheltered life; I was 20 years old before I learned that girls were not just soft boys.

Despite the difficulty of the challenge these days, I want to say a few good words about *love*.

Now I know love is a many-splendored thing. There are lots of dimensions of love. The ancient Greeks talked about love as *eros* — erotic associations. They also spoke of *philias* — brother or neighborly love. Then there was *agape* — the deepest kind of relationship. *Agape* goes deeper than mere sentiment and speaks of total commitment. It's the kind of love St. John was speaking about when he wrote in John 3:16… "God so loved the world, he gave his only begotten Son, that whoever believes in him shall not die but have everlasting life."

I'd like to lump all three of these forms of love together and make a Valentine's Day plea for some sheer ecstasy. Here's what I mean by ecstasy: "The abandonment of one's self to the wellbeing of one's beloved."

I hope each of us will find someone for ecstasy and intimacy.

This is a beautiful thing — a spiritual thing — love, romance, commitment. It is a gift of God. What is better than to care more for the welfare of someone else — your sweetheart — than you care for your own life?

I have noticed that *sweetheart-ery* sprouts early in life and is filled with hope and longing. A grandfather told me that his 2½-year-old grandson told his mother that he wanted to get married. She responded, "Oh, but you will have to wait until you are five years old." He said, "I'll just have to change my number."

One eight- year-old boy, speaking about why two particular people fall in love, said, "I think you're supposed to get shot with an arrow or something, but the rest of it isn't supposed to be too bad."

Love begins early, and then, if it is real, it flowers with beauty and grace, whimsy and delight and ends with loving, precious memories. In my ministry, I have conducted more than 1,000 funerals. Few things in life are more wonderful than to hear a surviving spouse speak with sheer gratitude about the ecstasy of life with a husband or wife — sweetheart — who, having gone on to be with God, has bathed his or her beloved with endearing, enduring memories.

So I say *run*, don't walk, to someone tonight. Take the hand of that someone you love and say so — *aloud*! If you are alone, find someone to love more than you love your own self. Grab a memory if you need to. Luxuriate in the abiding memory of that one whom you have loved right on into the arms of God.

I hope each of us will find someone for ecstasy and intimacy. I know it is not always easy. One morning I tried to get cuddly with my sweetheart of more than 50 years. She rebuffed my advances. I tried to apply some friendly pressure. It was raining and sleeting. So I said. "You may never see me again. I'll probably not survive this storm. I'll bet I get hit on the head by a big old hail ball and get killed to death!" As she pushed me out the door I wailed, "A hail ball about the size of a grapefruit, that's what it will be!" At least she called me at the office a couple of hours later to ask if that hail ball had hit me yet. So this is not easy, but still there is hope! ✦

Sitting in the swing with my sweetheart Judy

55

$\mathcal{S}$t. Peter at the Gate

One of the benefits of writing this divine stuff is that lots of folk send me loads of funny stuff. Through the years I have received thousands of tidbits, lists, jokes and stories from readers. I read them all. I toss many of them into the wastepaper basket because I have seen them so many times I wouldn't think of passing them on. Others I pass along to you dear readers in the hope that they will be new to you and that I can make some modest moral by repeating them. I try to give credit when I know the source.

Sometimes I see something I like but can't find the right occasion in which to use it. Those pieces I toss in a box and wait for some pretext to justify including in my column. This week I am going to share one such story that has been percolating in my "Someday File" for almost eight years. My main reason for printing this story is that I am getting so old and have had it so long, it has occurred to me that I might die before I ever get around to sharing it. Plus, I haven't been feeling too well lately.

The story: A fellow is at the Pearly Gates waiting to be admitted to heaven. Saint Peter is leafing through his Big Book to see if the guy is worthy of admission. The vigilant saint furrows his brow as he scans the pages. Then he says, "I can't find any record here that you ever did anything really good in your life. On the other hand, you never did anything really bad in your life either. I tell you what: If you can tell me one truly good deed you did in your life, I'll let you in."

The applicant thinks for a long moment and says, "Yes, sir there was this one time when I was driving down the highway and I saw a great bunch of bikers assaulting a poor motorist. I slowed down my car to see what was going on. Sure enough, there they were, about 50 of them, beating up this guy. Infuriated, I got out of my car and grabbed a tire iron out of my trunk. I walked straight up to the leader of the gang. He was a huge, tattooed guy with a studded leather jacket. He had a chain running from his nose to his ear. I could see right away he was not a deacon in the church.

"As I walked up to him the gang gathered, forming a circle around me. So I ripped the leader's chain off his face and smashed him over his head with the tire iron. Then I turned to the crowd and yelled, 'Leave this poor fellow alone! You're all a bunch of sick, depraved animals! Go home before I teach you all a lesson in pain!'"

Well, St. Peter was very impressed. He began again to leaf through his book. "Really? When did this incident take place?"

The hopeful pilgrim breathed a sigh of relief and replied, "About two minutes ago."

Now I am a politically correct parson. I don't mean to cast any aspersions against bikers, tattooed folk or anybody else. Some of my best friends are tattooed preacher bikers. Also, I'm aware of the questionable theology one could infer from this tale. Our good works are not the secret to entering the heavenly realm. I know that.

I can't think of a good way to follow this yarn with a moral that you earnest folk can apply to your lives. Oh, I could warn you about trying to get through the Pearly Gates with a tire iron in your hand. St. Peter is too sharp-eyed and savvy to let that go unnoticed. And it goes without saying that no one can sneak a checkbook over the heavenly portals. I guess the best advice I can give is to suggest that you approach the great old saint like the best of us Methodists — with a covered dish, a casserole, in your hands! ✦

56

*M*oving Ministers

Well, folks, it's that time of the year again when the topic on the minds of most Methodists is whether or not they are likely to have a change of minister down at the church. When I was a United Methodist District Superintendent, a big part of my job was to help the Bishop assign ministers to churches. We believe we've got a good system for dealing with such things as the assignment of pastors. Of course, it's not perfect but until a better one comes along, we stick with it. And we will continue to believe God uses it to the Kingdom's advantage. That's actually no small achievement, even for God, since we pastors often have our own personal ambitions and family responsibilities that affect where we would prefer to serve. However, we are pledged to go where we are sent. Almost always we are well received and are delighted to be where we are assigned.

Every denomination has its own way of deploying its ministerial personnel. However, I'm guessing that some of the same dynamics are at play in any system when it comes to assessing candidates for pastoral leadership.

Here are some reasons some folk from Bible times might have a hard time getting a job in a church these days:

1. Adam. A good man but had problems with his wife. They ate fruit, something nutritionists say we all should do. Also they enjoyed walking around "nekked" in the garden.

2. Noah. Former pastorate of 120 years produced no converts. He was known to favor big boats. Brave man — took a cruise with a boatload of animals and a pair of hungry fleas.

3. Abraham. Offered to share his wife with a prominent man. Apparently unstable. Spent years moving around without knowing where he was going.

4. Moses. Couldn't speak well because of a stuttering problem. Once killed a man. Had an interracial marriage.

5. Solomon. A wise man but had too many wives for the typical parsonage.

6. David. Great singer but had an affair with his neighbor's wife after he had her husband killed.

7. John. To begin with, he dressed weirdly and ate bugs. He was a Baptist, so he wouldn't fit in just anywhere.

8. Peter. Talented, but too much of a hothead. Prone to lying and occasional violence.

9. Paul. Smart, but hard on some folk. Preaching was apparently boring. He put one fellow to sleep with his sermon and caused him to fall out a window. Long-winded and preached all night.

10. The Virgin Mary. Pure, but she's … well … a *she*.

11. Jesus. He's available, but his price may be too much for lots of us.

Well, there you have it. Finding a perfect pastor is difficult. It's no bowl of cherries for a pastor who is looking for a perfect church, either. We take what God and our various church systems offer us and make the best of each other. And usually that's not bad, not bad at all. ✦

57

The Quarter-Acre Universe

Our backyard is a quarter-acre universe. It is a place where dramas of life are played out daily. The flora and fauna are endlessly fascinating. From our glass-enclosed sunroom and from our outdoor deck, Judy and I observe the ebb and flow of life in that universe.

Some plants flourish and others struggle and fail. My little fig tree was barren of fruit a couple of years ago, so I cursed it after the fashion of Jesus. Roses have a hard time there. Little cherry tomatoes love it there. They are Edenic in their profusion. Hostas thrive in wide variety there. Animals scamper about in profusion. Squirrels, chipmunks, voles and birds of all sorts are abundant. And our outdoor cat, Liberty, and dog, Little Bit, are out there too.

We human types are welcome there, but we are like aliens from some other universe. It is a domain that truly belongs to them. This past weekend was a poignant time for us as we witnessed a grand drama in this little world.

On Saturday morning I stepped out to greet and feed Little Bit and Liberty. I came upon a major crisis: Little Bit was in obvious distress.

He was standing in the middle of the yard, struggling to stand up but also unable to lie down. He was unable to walk. He could only wobble in place. It was shocking and painful to watch. He is almost deaf now, but as I came close enough for him to hear me, he could not respond to me.

It being a weekend, the animal clinic was closed. So we administered as much comfort as we knew how to give. We gently caressed him. We offered soothing words. We tried food and water, but he could not accept it. We thought perhaps he had suffered a stroke. We thought maybe the inevitable had arrived. He is, after all, 16 years old. We have all heard that one dog's year is equivalent to seven years of human life. That makes him 112 years old.

We kept vigil with him. I remembered how, when I was near death for weeks four years ago, he stayed indoors and constantly alert at my bedside. I never looked down at him, night or day, and found him doing anything but looking up at me. After my crisis passed, he was eager to return to his outdoor haunts. I will always remain grateful for his vigilance and love for me.

During the day we noticed remarkable behavior from Liberty the cat. She began to frequently brush against him. She stayed near him — something she would never have done voluntarily before. She meowed often and was uncharacteristically fidgety and restless.

We human types are welcome there, but we are like aliens from some other universe.

This was strange behavior because Little Bit and Liberty have tormented each other all their lives. They are the same age, and they have grown up together. He has chased her incessantly for years. He forced us to feed her atop a picnic table because he wouldn't let her eat in peace if he could reach her. They have had a sibling rivalry for 112 years! But now she knows something is terribly wrong.

As the day wore on, we noticed slow but definite improvement in his condition. After a few hours he was able to move steadily. He could eat a few bites of food. The crisis seemed to have passed. And the next day he experienced some of the same symptoms, but they were less severe and shorter in duration. We hope tomorrow will be a better day for him and for Liberty and for us too.

Watching this and feeling the solemnity of it, I have not been able to shake from my mind the words of the familiar children's song written by Cecil F. Alexander in 1848:

> "All things bright and beautiful,
> All creatures great and small,
> All things wise and wonderful:
> The Lord God made them all."

Those words seem so obviously true in our small quarter-acre universe. A look out the window upon our larger universe makes it seem, sadly, less obviously so. ✦

58

$\mathcal{L}$ittle Bit and Liberty

Last week I wrote about the health crisis of Little Bit, our 16-year-old dog. That's 112 human years. We had discovered him in distress on Saturday. He appeared to have suffered a stroke. He couldn't walk and couldn't eat. But we were buoyed up by a steady recovery of the ability to walk as the day wore on. Then he made slow but obvious progress day after day. He drank water but had no appetite for food. Finally the end came on Valentine's Day morning. Apparently his heart just stopped. He showed no obvious signs of pain during those last days and nights.

I told last week about the surprising behavior of Liberty, our cat, who sensed Little Bit's distress and who fretted over him. This surprised us because he had sometimes annoyed her terribly. He chased her endlessly. And he kept her off his turf. Now, in his time of extremity, her emotions were obviously on edge. We observed her grooming him. She caressed him with her paws. She was restless when she could not see him. She paced the yard, meowing constantly. As I dug a grave for him in the sunny spot where he loved to lie in the mornings, she sat a few feet away and watched until I finished digging. Then she followed me toward the house, meowing and rubbing against the legs of the picnic table and my own leg. She seemed to yearn for some kind, any kind, of touch. She is the same age as Little Bit. They grew up together. We never had even an inkling that they cared for each other.

> *We* never had even an inkling that they cared for each other.

Moments later, I carried Little Bit in my arms to the grave. I had wrapped him in a little red blanket given him by our daughter Susannah. He spent his last living days and nights at the foot of her bed, and upon that familiar blanket he had died. Liberty followed and sat at arm's length to watch as I buried him in a little patch of daffodils and daylilies. I returned to the house but watched from a window as she continued to sit motionless. After several minutes she stood and walked over to the mound and sat again; then she lay there. Eventually she disappeared from view. Several times later in the day she repeated the pattern.

I have learned a lot from these family pets. I have learned that there was a far more complex relationship between these little animals than I had imagined. As for Liberty the cat, I now know she was far more emotional than she had ever revealed before. She has always lived up to her name. She lives outside. She is free and guards her liberty with determination. She has always been stoic and a loner, I thought. Now I have discovered in her a quality of personality that I have not seen in all these years. And Little Bit, who was always a little bundle of bluster, full of bark but almost no bite, must have loved not only me but her also. I had thought him unkind to her because he pestered her so. Perhaps she learned over time that he was mostly a tease.

This experience leaves me with the strengthened conclusion that all of God's creation is precious and to be treasured by good stewards. I've always known this, of course. But I'm stirred to be more attentive to this truth because of these two furry senior citizens of the animal kingdom. You who have pets understand how we feel. You who don't have pets are missing some of God's blessings. So at our house we say, adopt a pet to learn from and to share love. ✦

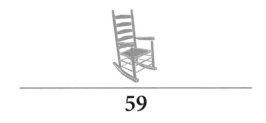

59

*C*ar Trouble

Friends, I have bad news. You know me: I usually try to look on the bright side. Maybe by the time I get to the end of this blessed blurb today, I'll be over my depression. I hope so.

Here's my problem. My car engine died this week. My beloved and I were on the way to church when it just quit running. She was driving at the time, but I don't blame this on her. She's a good driver and does most of the driving nowadays because my driving makes her nervous.

My only complaint about her driving is that she drives too slowly. At my age, I need to go as fast as the law allows if I'm going to get all the stuff done that I want to do.

Anyhow, we were cruising up the interstate, and it just quit. So I called AAA. An hour and 20 minutes, later the tow truck arrived and towed me to a garage while a friend took my darlin' home. After a while and a couple of hundred dollars, I learned my problem was greater than that shop could handle, so the next day I had my comatose car towed to another shop.

At my age, I need to go as fast as the law allows if I'm going to get all the stuff done that I want to do.

Five days later I learned that I needed another engine. A thingy inside the engine had broken and ruined some gizmos, and I was up the proverbial creek without a piston — so to speak. By the time you read this, I will be purring along with my replacement engine. It won't be a new one because a new engine costs more than my car is worth. But I only have 130,000 miles on it. I can't give up on it now. I put 364,000 miles on my last car. It isn't that I'm cheap about cars. I simply like to get full value out of things.

This automotive adventure has put me in a sentimental frame of mind. I wish I still had my first automobile — a 1950 Studebaker Champion. Most of you dear readers are not old enough to remember Studebakers. They were weird-looking cars whose front and rear ends were very similar. You could hardly tell whether they were coming or going.

My Studebaker had a funky look about it, and for a teenage high-school idol like me, it was definitely not a cool car. It was a good car, however, and in great shape. It had been owned by an older maiden second cousin of mine, who had bought it new and driven it mostly to church. It was forest green and upholstered in a fabric that looked and felt like grayish mouse fur. I know what you're thinking. Made my skin crawl too. But I bought it for $95. Nowadays people pay more than that for a decent ticket to a professional sporting event. I don't pay that much because, as I said earlier, I like to get full value out of things — like money.

Alas, like many foolish lads, I got rid of that really good car as soon as I could get a loan and I bought a little sports car. My sweetheart didn't like it because it was a two-seater and we couldn't carry along friends when we went places. But that was one of the reasons I liked it. I didn't want anybody going out with us!

My little sports car was so easy on gas that I never needed much more than fifty cents for fuel to get anywhere we wanted to go on a Saturday night. This was fortunate for me because I never had much more than $2.50 in those days. I drove the car for several months on a dead battery. It was so lightweight I would just park on an incline, push it off and jump in whenever I needed to start it. Ah, the good old days!

Now I've got to replace my engine. I'm glad I have that car. It's a blessing. But I wish I still had that old Studebaker. The memory of it is worth more than the $95 I paid for it. And I wish I still had my little old sports car. I'd like to take my sweetheart for a ride in it once more. Now, after more than 50 years of marriage, I think she's content to ride just with me; no passengers invited. ✦

60

*B*ring Cash

Last week Travis Stewart from over at Davidson, North Carolina, died. How I loved Travis. When we were together, we were a dangerous pair! We were loud and loved good fun. She was one of the most devout persons I've ever known.

I became her minister in the early 1980s. Her husband, Watson, was very ill at the time. After a long and courageous fight against cancer, Watson died. When I sat down with Travis to plan his funeral, she told me that they had been visiting New Orleans once and had witnessed a traditional funeral parade with the marching band and the coffin moving through the streets. Watson remarked that he would like some of that kind of music at his funeral when his time came. She wanted to honor his wish. So we did.

I arranged to have Fleet Green, a Charlotte musical legend, and his Dixieland band assist with the service. They sat in the chancel, dressed in white pants, red-and-white striped vests and straw hats. I instructed him to begin playing at 20 minutes before the appointed hour. Additionally, I asked him to keep an eye on me for a signal to quit playing when it was time to start the service.

Well, folks, the people kept streaming in, and I kept motioning for Fleet and his boys to keep playing. Soon more than a thousand people filled the sanctuary.

Finally, I held up two fingers to indicate that he play two more pieces. I saw panic in his eyes. Then we all heard the familiar notes of "(Won't You Come Home) Bill Bailey." *Twice*! Fleet and his band had run out of all the religious music they knew. They were doing the best they could! Travis, the widow, loved it! At the end of the funeral, as we marched to a reception in her late husband's memory, we sang "When the Saints Go Marching In."

Travis has now taken her place among the saints who from their labors rest. Once again we sang "When the Saints Go Marching In." What memories! After Travis Stewart's joyous memorial service, one of our mutual friends, who wishes to remain anonymous, told me the following story.

"One of her friends died recently in a city which shall remain unidentified. Suffice to say, it was a city that does not observe the funeral customs common to the South. There was a small private graveside service. The widow of the deceased wanted to remain there until her beloved husband's coffin was finally lowered into the grave. When the priest's remarks were ended and the benediction given, there was an awkward pause.

"After a few minutes, the attendant from the cemetery informed the widow that he would not lower the coffin into the grave until he was paid. Well, this was an unexpected development, to say the least. The widow looked into her purse only to discover that she had no cash! So she asked if he would accept a credit card. He declined the credit card. Then, with the coffin still sitting there, she asked if he would accept a check.

"The semi-compassionate fellow, eager to be helpful, replied, 'Yes.' He then said, 'May I please see your driver's license?'"

Dearly beloved, the times, they are a'changin'. Nowadays, remember to bring along some cash!

It hasn't been many years since Southern culture featured funeral processions to the cemeteries. Family and friends would follow the hearse slowly with headlights burning and small pennants waving. Police escorts led the way and stopped traffic at intersections while the parade proceeded without interruption. Oncoming traffic would pause out of respect for the deceased. These things are becoming less common.

Some cities now prohibit such interruptions of the flow of traffic. Speed on roadways makes such things dangerous, they say, and police are needed to fight crime. Therefore it is too expensive to keep to old customs.

Still, an old geezer minister like this humble parson sometimes pines for the days when we all doffed our hats out of respect for the departed. Now we don't even remove our hats when we sit down for dinner. Alas! ✦

61

You Take Your Chances

I am writing today from New Orleans, one of the South's great cities. Two blocks from my hotel is Harrah's Casino. Harrah's has a casino in Cherokee, North Carolina too. State lotteries are popping up like briars all over the South. On principle, I'm against gambling. I believe people ought to work for what they've got. Gambling undercuts some of our basic spiritual values too.

But you know how it is. Just because I have principles doesn't mean temptation isn't here. I am glad to report that I have not yielded to temptation and visited the casino. I haven't bought any lottery tickets either.

It is tempting to attribute my behavior to some kind of moral excellence. However, I confess I am driven mostly by fear. Each time I am tempted, I think to myself: "If I do this, it will be just my luck to win a million dollars. Then everyone will learn of my transgression."

On the other hand, I know what I'd do if I had a million dollars: I'd pay my bills as long as it lasts. What would you do if you were to win a million bucks? One woman who did win a million was asked what she would do with it. She said, "Well, I think I'll get my washing machine fixed." A farmer who hit the jackpot said he planned to keep on farming so long as his million lasted.

I had a parishioner once who, on her honeymoon cruise, hit the jackpot at the slot machine in the ship's casino. On the way home, she began thinking about the historic Methodist opposition to gambling. So the next Sunday she put a sock full of quarters in the offering plate. She explained in a note that her conscience was causing her to give her winnings to the Lord. She ended her note by telling me that I could keep the socks. (The note was stuffed, along with the other sock, in with the coins.)

I told the congregation about the donation and announced that we were glad for all kinds of contributions. I said we even accepted "plastic"—meaning credit cards. Actually, we didn't accept credit cards, but I thought it was a cute quip. Well, the offering plate the next Sunday contained an envelope addressed to me. Inside was perhaps the most useless gift I've ever received: a plastic comb.

One of the ironies of modern life in many states nowadays is that gambling is touted as the best way to finance public programs important to the civilizing process… public education, for example. It just doesn't make sense to me that so-called "sin taxes" on things like alcoholic beverages or tobacco products or revenue from gambling is any way to build a healthy society. There's something about such a scheme that just doesn't compute. However, it isn't hard to compute the social costs of such a strategy.

It is tempting to attribute my behavior to some kind of moral excellence.

So I'm writing not so much to keep you from buying a lottery ticket as to give you fair warning. If I find out you've suddenly got a million dollars, I'm going to come looking for what, unless you've worked for it, belongs to the Lord. And I plan to confiscate your socks for myself. ✦

62

*T*he Ten Commandments

The old comedian W.C. Fields, when asked if he read the Bible, said, "I do read the Bible but only to look for loopholes." A reader of the Bible won't find any loopholes. The folly of such an idea is what makes the comment funny. On the other hand, the Bible is a book of infinitely practical insights and helpful advice. It contains all you need for the good life and all we need for a civilized world.

You won't find this particular biblical advice on the wall at the schoolhouse or the courthouse any more, but it is still among the best wisdom in the history of the world. It is arranged in ten parts. The first four parts have to do with gods:

- First, don't let any other gods outrank the Lord God of Israel.
- Second, don't manufacture anything that you might be tempted to worship.
- Third, don't misuse the name of God. In other words, don't invoke the name of God inappropriately.
- Fourth, be serious about how you use time. Give one seventh of it to God.

Those commandments are about how people who are God-minded ought to behave. Folk who don't believe in the God of the Bible seem especially troubled about those who do. One would think people who don't believe in the existence of God would be indifferent about such things but they certainly aren't.

The next six commandments are all directed towards helping people live together in society:

- Treat your mother and father with honor and respect.
- Don't commit murder.
- If you are married, don't mess around with someone else's husband or wife.
- Don't take stuff that doesn't belong to you.
- Don't lie about your neighbors.
- Don't desire anything that belongs to your neighbor.

What thoughtful, intelligent person would deny that these principles contribute to a just and civilized society? Who would advocate the reverse of these social guidelines? Yet some folk spend enormous amounts of energy, time and money arguing that exposure of these ideas in public places is a danger to the republic. Some such persons are simply mischief-makers trying to confound the devout. Others are publicity seekers looking for public attention. Of course, some who want all-things-religious driven behind closed doors are very sincere. However, no matter the motives, at the end of the day these exercises are as futile as searching the Bible for loopholes. ✦

63

*P*olitics on His Mind

I saw my old buddy, Cicero Fudd, last week. He's a crotchety old geezer, very opinionated. Sometimes he is actually insightful. Ever since he learned he bears the name of an ancient philosopher, he mostly sits on his front porch in a rocking chair. He chews tobacco, spits a lot and keeps a vigilant eye on his old car, which sits on blocks in his front yard. And he ponders things.

Cicero had politics on his mind when I stopped by to see him. I could see that he was levelheaded on this particular morning because the tobacco juice was running out of both sides of his mouth. I asked why he seemed a little down in his emotions. He replied, "Well, you know I'm an old man now, and on most days I don't feel good anymore. I'm worried that some politicians want to end Social Security and Medicare. I know they say it won't affect people my age. (I think Cicero is in his mid 80s.) But people who are younger than 55 are gonna get old too.

"I wouldn't be alive today if it weren't for Social Security and Medicare. I'm worried about my grandchildren's future. I don't think they will get to live as long as I have. If some politicians get their way, our health care is going to be rolled back to what it was in my great-grandpa's day."

I asked him what he meant by that comment. He noticed a mouse coming out from under his porch and, quick as a wink, spat a golden stream and scored a direct hit on little Mickey, who disappeared in a flash. Then he told me a story, the facts of which I find doubtful, but the point of which I find intriguing. You be the judge. Here's the tale.

"Great-grandpa said he knew a man many years ago who fell off his horse. This was back before automobiles became commonplace. Well, when he fell from his horse, it spooked the animal and the steed kicked him in the face. What's more, it kicked his nose off. There was no doctor anywhere near. But there was a woman who was known as a good seamstress in the community. So she sewed the nose back on the victim's face. Her stitchery was fine — small, even stitches. However, she made a serious mistake. She sewed the nose on upside down.

"Despite the error, the nose worked pretty well. The main problem with it was that when it rained, the nose would fill up with water. One winter the man was caught out in a sudden icy storm. His nose filled with water and froze. He caught a terrible head cold. When the storm passed, the temperature rose and the ice thawed. The man sneezed and blew his hat off! Then the cold wind blew back in and the head cold moved down into his chest and he died."

Cicero paused for dramatic effect and hit an empty sardine can 10 feet away with a missile of chewed tobacco. Then he asked, "Do we want to go back to those old days of no Social Security and no help with health care?"

I asked my old buddy, "Well, Cicero, we've got a big national debt. How are we going to pay for these things?" His eyes flashed and he snapped back, "In the first place we ought to put in jail every politician who became a multimillionaire *after* getting elected to office. That's where I'd start.

In the second place, we ought to let a lot of people out of jail who are a danger to nobody anymore. That'll save a boatload of money. Finally, we can quit some of these wars. With the money we save we'll be able to pay off our country's mortgage quicker than my great-grandpa paid off the mortgage on the farm."

I knew Cicero has cut back on his heart medicine to save money. As his face reddened, I began to worry. I didn't want to agitate him further. So I excused myself and went back to work. ✦

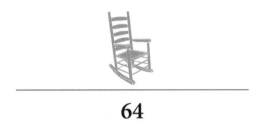

64

*F*eeling Thankful

I won't lie to you: I begin to get soggy around the gizzard at this time every year. Thanksgiving is just around the corner. Sentimental guy that I am, I am thinking about all the things for which I am grateful. Today I'm thinking about the women in my life.

A few days ago I marked the memory of my mother and mother-in-law. They both died on the 12th of October, a year apart. It was more than a decade ago, but my memories of them are as vivid as ever. I still get a lump in my throat as if it were yesterday. I'm also thinking about another gal I adored. On her 45th birthday, our oldest daughter, Janice, died. Tears still flow.

But I have lots of joy about the women in my life. I have an amazing daughter, two great daughters-in-law and four fabulous granddaughters, all whom I admire and love dearly. Judy, my wife of over 50 years, I love more with each passing day. (I warned you. I'm sentimental!)

My sweet daughter-in-law Christie sent me a note this week entitled "Why Men Prefer Dogs Instead of Wives." I don't know where she got this list but here it is. This is why men prefer dogs:

(1) The later you are, the more excited your dogs are to see you.

(2) Dogs don't notice if you call them by another dog's name.

(3) Dogs like it if you leave things on the floor.

(4) A dog's parents never visit.

(5.) Dogs agree that you have to raise your voice to get your point across.

(6) You never have to wait for a dog; they're ready to go 24 hours a day.

(7) Dogs find you amusing when you're drunk.

(8) Dogs like to go hunting and fishing.

(9) A dog will never wake you up at night to ask, "If I died, would you get another dog?"

(10) Dogs like to ride in the back of a pickup truck. And last but not least...

(11) If a dog leaves, it won't take half your stuff.

Now, these items are unlikely to achieve the status of domestic proverbs alongside the Book of Proverbs in the Bible or the wisdom of *Poor Richard's Almanac*. But they are funny anyhow.

For one thing, they point up some of the familiar foibles of the male persuasion. They remind us husbands of what louts we can be sometimes. They also give attention to us all of some of the potholes in domestic life that cause blowouts on the tires of marriage.

For many folk, humor emerges out of minor irritations and human pain, but I don't think that's true of Christie's list. She knows David adores her. And she and David both love dogs. They have two strikingly beautiful dogs, a Blue Tick hound, Rufus, and a half German shepherd, half wolf, Riley. They are huge, playful dogs. Still, I'm guessing Christie, in good fun, could write a personal list of "Why Wives Prefer Dogs Instead of Husbands."

Romantics sometimes speak of shouting their love from mountaintops. But what about those who live nowhere near a mountain? The great thing about real love is that it works in any geographical setting. From the icebergs of Alaska to the Great Dismal Swamp of coastal Virginia and North Carolina, love works. From the flat Great Plains to the liquid Louisiana bayou, love works.

The great thing about real love is that it works in any geographical setting.

People who love the Bible turn to Proverbs 31 to find a paean to the excellent wife and mother. On Mother's Day they dust off the Book and read again the familiar words of tribute. The picture emerges of the super woman. She is the model of industry, generous to a fault, kind, wise, loving and dignified. Almost every mother is all of these things. But I'm shouting cheers, from Thanksgiving to forever, for *all* you gals, not just mothers!

Now, back to the dogs. Everyone could become more endearing to others by displaying some of the attributes of a canine! An occasional playful bark or an act of affectionate obedience — what's not to love about that? Or a romp on the lawn. Or a protective display of vigilance. Or even a rare display of heroism. We adore our dogs — we husbands *and* wives. And we laugh at the extremes to which our affection extends. The best thing, though, is that we love each other — thank God! ✦

65

$\mathcal{S}$earching the Attic

For as long as I can remember, I have scribbled notes on scraps of paper and tossed them into desk drawers, bedside-table drawers, dashboard compartments of cars and mostly storage boxes. I've been cleaning out my attic recently and looking through the stuff. The topics are as varied as one can imagine. Lots of them make little sense to me now, after lying there all these years. I've discarded a foothill if not a small mountain of the stuff.

There must have been some reason I thought some of it was worth keeping, but not anymore. For instance, I once started a commentary on the animal kingdom. "A camel is a horse designed by a Methodist committee." And "An elephant is a mouse built to government specifications." I didn't go much farther on that project, partly because I am almost certain that I heard that material from someone else but I don't know who. I figure if I'm going to plagiarize something, it ought to be better than that.

Some of my notes mark historical events. Here's a note I wrote in December 1983 on the death of the great Spanish artist Juan Miro. He said, "I never dream when I'm sleeping — only when I'm awake." I know what he means.

Here's a note I made to myself while spending a summer preaching in Australia back in the '70s. There is, in the Australian consciousness, a wonderful myth that I love. Somewhere out beyond the horizon is the charred stump of a long-dead, burned-out tree. North, south, east, west — it doesn't matter which direction you choose, the black stump is there. No one knows what kind of tree it was or how long it has been there. However, it is there marking the boundary of meaningful space. No one has ever seen it but it is there. When an Aussie wants to speak of the biggest or smallest, smartest or most ignorant, prettiest or ugliest of anything or anybody, he uses the phrase, "This side of the black stump." That little phrase rules out all comparison. Beyond the black stump there is nothing but an infinity of desert dunes where no trees grow. That is an intriguing image to ponder.

Lots of these fragments are theological. I have no recollection of the context in which I wrote this, but I think it's a keeper: "Your sin is not forgiven until it is ended. Don't ask God to forgive what you are unwilling to quit doing." When I was very ill, I wrote on a paper napkin, "I don't know why I have this illness, but somehow I know God is trusting me with it."

I don't know why I have this illness, but somehow I know God is trusting me with it.

After hearing a college professor tell this story, I made this note: "The young girl was so badly misshapen I could hardly bear to look at her. I asked her why she was in college. She said, 'When I was born the doctor told my mother I would never walk. But my mother pulled me across the floor, forcing me to try, three times a day. I cried. I thought my mother did not love me. I later learned that three times a day, my mother cried too.'"

The daily news often provides a report about something too good to pass by... like the report on the woman who received her certification to do CPR. On her way home a flash flood deluged her town. Suddenly she saw a man face down in the water. She stopped her car and ran to him, turned him over on his back and began to administer mouth-to-mouth resuscitation. He struggled free and shouted, "Lady, I don't know what you're doing but I'm trying to unstop this sewer!"

As I rummage through these bits and pieces, I'm reminded of what fun I've had along the way. I've laughed a lot and cried some too. I've learned loads and taught a little here and there. One of the great discoveries is that at the rate I'm going, it will take me another 50 years to sift through this stuff in my attic. I hope you've got an attic of good memories too! ✦

66

*W*ar Touches Our Family Once More
Published: December 2009

Today is the first Sunday of Advent, the beginning of the traditional time of year when Christians are reminded of the birth of Jesus and the biblical promise of his Second Coming. It is a time of anticipation for followers of Christ. Every year this blessed season arrives in a new context. Times change and our challenges are always evolving. Some things are getting better for the human family. Other things remain the same. Sometimes the whole Earth seems to groan under the weight of profound human woes.

This morning at worship, the following words were part of my prayer with the congregation:

"Again this year, as so often in the past, we pray to you, God, against a backdrop of wars and conflicts in this world. Prince of Peace, Lord, raise up and empower wise peacemakers. Grant, O God, that we will waste no more human lives on the altar of human sin, arrogance, ambition and pride. Make us learn to pour our resources into the advancement of civilization rather than into the pockets of those who profit off conflict and human misery."

This is an especially poignant week for our family. On Friday our oldest grandson, John White, will complete his U.S. Army basic training at Fort Benning, Georgia. He will spend a brief time in Germany, then he will be deployed to Afghanistan. We now join those other families whose daily prayers will intensify immensely. It is a relatively small group of Americans touched so directly by war this Christmas. Most of us read the news with a generalized detachment and a shrug: "It doesn't much affect us." But for us few who have loved ones at risk, a different emotion applies.

> *We* yearn for the Prince of Peace in this Advent and Christmas season to do his work in this world.

Our family has a long history of military service to America in every war dating back to the Revolutionary War. In the Civil War ours, like many others, was a divided family. Most of our ancestors were in the Union Army, but some served in the Confederate Army. One of our great-great-great-grandfathers died in a Confederate prison camp. When the nation called, our family has been quick to answer. We honor the men and women from our family who have served and continue to serve.

Still I detest war. Those who cause wars to arise violate most of the Ten Commandments and most of the principles of civilized behavior.

So often the origins of war are found in aggressive ambitions against neighbors. Greed and covetousness power the conflicts. The urge to control others is a motivating force. The list goes on and on: racial and cultural enmity, national arrogance, religious pride, ignorance, bigotry and hate.

So we yearn for the Prince of Peace in this Advent and Christmas season to do his work in this world. We want no more families to suffer the grief of the loss of a son or daughter to war. We want no more loss of innocent people at the hands of murderous barbarians. We want all people to sleep in safety. We want all children to be healthy and well fed, educated and happy. We want all old people to be at ease in their final years. We want justice and peace for everyone.

Our grandson, John

We love our John. He is dear to our hearts. We are proud of him. And we pray for him and all others who follow a sense of duty into the service of peace. We pray that God will protect them and that they will always be on the side of what is right and just in this world. ✦

67

$\mathcal{I}$deas New and Old

My beloved and I had a small group of our dear friends in for lunch last week. They are all vivacious, energetic senior citizens. I got inspired by their presence to make a proposal. In retrospect, maybe I was carried away by my enthusiasm and reached too far. I proposed that we, this band of buddies, go trick-or-treating this Halloween. My motion failed for lack of a second.

Some may have feared what treats might have been dropped into our goody bags. Oh, we might have collected a few of the conventional treats that regularly show up when the kids go out on Halloween: Tootsie Pops, Hershey Kisses, bubble gum, etc. Probably we would have found items more stereotypical of our senior status: Fixodent, Geritol, Beano, etc. I reckon some items would not have been so useful to us: taffy, caramels and other chewy sweets. In any case, my Halloween idea did not catch fire, so I quietly allowed it to expire.

This episode reminded me of my proposal to Judy when we were discussing how to celebrate our 50th wedding anniversary. I suggested we go bungee jumping. Her reaction caused me to briefly fear she would seek an annulment of our marriage.

I have always been full of ideas. I think all of them have been pretty good ones. However, I may have sometimes been lulled into the mistaken notion that *all* my ideas are *great* ones. Honestly, some of my brainstorms have been duds. Actually I've always believed that we need to have a reasonably high EQ to be successful in life. What is an EQ? It's an Error Quotient. It's to help us profit from our bad ideas. The EQ is a cousin to the IQ, or Intelligence Quotient which reminds us that our brainpower is important. Both EQ and IQ are necessary in our toolkits for good living.

I figure if we don't experience a few fizzles with our big ideas, we are not risking enough for God's sake. This is especially true in the church. Someone once observed, "The seven last words of the church are: "We never done it that way before." I think we should consider, "Why not?" We ought to *reward* risking for God! That means feeling good about an occasional fizzle. Many religious folk tend to be risk averse, afraid to stretch lest they fail. So they become dream-busters when new things are proposed in the work and ministry of the church.

Equally dangerous to progress is the belief by some people that a once-failed idea is a forever-bad idea. "Forget that. We tried that once and it didn't work out." How often have we heard that? Sometimes a good idea just happens to arise at an inopportune point in time.

"In the fullness of time" is an old biblical phrase that reminds us that there are two types of time. First, there's *chronos* time, which means chronological time. Then there's *kairos* time, God's time, when there is a richness to the moment and extraordinary things happen. It was a *kairos,* or opportune, "fullness" moment when Jesus appeared on the great stage of human history.

If you want to be a great leader, find and disprove a treasured axiom. God can use you as a leader if you will work on disproving the idea that

> *I figure if we don't experience a few fizzles with our big ideas, we are not risking enough for God's sake.*

change is bad and to be resisted. The *nature* of God is unchanging; that is true. But the *business* of God is redemptive change. Personal spirituality is mostly the quest for two things: (1) *Self awareness.* Everyone needs to know who God has created in her or him. (2) *Divine vision.* How is God changing one to complete one's destiny? We may try to stand still but God keeps working on us. We are perpetual construction sites where remodeling sometimes slows but never stops until we meet the Master Builder face to face. ✦

68

*P*artisan Politics

Recent elections and the workings of national government have gotten me to thinking about the origins of modern political partisanship. And about how little politics has changed through the years. Consider this: Real partisan politics started in 1057 A.D. in Coventry, England, when Lady Godiva, wife of Leofric, Earl of Mercia, made her famous protest against high taxes by riding naked through the town. Here's what happened:

Godiva and Leofric, being devoutly religious people and having become affluent because of their success in the mutton business, decided to build a monastery for the training of clergy to care for souls. It was a simple structure, built from wattle and daub with a thatched roof. Still, it was the most prominent building in town.

One thing led to another, and Leofric, philanthropic gentleman that he was becoming, began to take a growing role in the public affairs of the town. Before long he was given responsibility for the financial needs of the community. As the public projects multiplied, the need for more tax revenue, grew and Leofric levied taxes left and right. It got to the point he even taxed manure!

Lady G. nagged him so much about taxes he finally told her he would cut them if she would ride a horse naked through town in the bright light of day. So, undoubtedly to his great surprise, she did it! There she went, right through town in broad daylight. The people lined the streets as she passed by. On one side the onlookers watched with understandable curiosity. However, she was riding sidesaddle, as any proper lady would. So the people watching from the other side of the street were cheering wildly and shouting, "Hooray for our side!" This is how partisanship began.

Even the most partisan Republican has to admit the Democrats haven't tried to tax manure.

Of course, taxes continue to be a point of debate in partisan politics. I'm glad the Republicans have resisted demonstrating their devotion to lower taxes by shucking off their clothes and riding through town stark "nekked." On the other hand, even the most partisan Republican has to admit the Democrats haven't tried to tax manure.

I'm registered as an independent voter. This enables me to have good friends in both of our major parties. And, of course, this allows me to grumble and complain about both parties whenever I wish. This helps me maintain a measure of dispassionate objectivity when the debate and rivalry gets especially heated. Now don't get me wrong: I'm in favor of party politics. But there are some vocations, including my own, in which it is helpful to the larger cause if a preacher keeps out of the campaign fray.

I was once the pastor to both the chair of the county Republican Party and the chair of the county Democrats. Part of my job was to encourage them both in their willingness to give political leadership. My other job was to remind them that both Democrats and Republicans are sinners. I have noticed that when religion and politics get mixed in together, the politically partisan tail often begins to wag the theological dog.

I don't want to be the religious counterpart to the judge who presided over the famous cannibalism trial of J.W. Packer. In 1873 Packer got caught in a Colorado blizzard and wound up eating some of his buddies. The judge betrayed his partisan feelings when he leaned over the bench and sternly rebuked the defendant: "Packer, you depraved Republican son-of-a-so-and-so! They wuz only five Democrats in Hinsdale County and you et all five of 'em!" ✦

69

*O*ne-Liners

My friend Debi Nelson sends me lots of cute stuff to tickle my funny bone. Recently she sent some "Christian One-Liners." Some are funny; some are wise; some are cautionary; some are inspiring. Try some of these on for size.

"Don't let your worries get the best of you. Remember, Moses started out as a basket case." Now, this probably ought to head the list of Jewish one-liners since it refers to the story of the birth of the great

Hebrew leader. But Moses belongs to Christians too. He's one of the heroes of the Old Testament. He truly was a basket case at times. Once he killed an Egyptian in a moment of anger. Still he was greatly used as an instrument of God. Moses is a reminder of how flawed people can be tremendous servants of humanity and of God. The Bible is replete with such people.

Here's another one-liner: "Many folks want to serve God. But only as advisers." An old friend told me once about attending a prayer meeting. He said the participants sat in a circle and they each, in turn, offered a prayer to God. He said by the time it came his turn to pray to God, they had loaded the Divinity with so many requests, directions of things they wanted God to do and words of advice, he refused to pray. He said, "God already has enough to do. I pass!"

One-liner: "We are called to be witnesses, not lawyers or judges." Of course, this refers not to secular life but to spirituality. One of the great temptations for religious folk is to revel in debates about fine points of theological law. It's awfully easy to win a debate and lose the point. Who among us isn't guilty of having been judgmental about people with whom we see things differently? Wouldn't it be nice if religious folk would mostly stick with simply telling others what they have seen and heard from God?

Moses is a reminder of how flawed people can be tremendous servants of humanity and of God.

Here's a goodie: "People are funny: they want the front of the bus, the middle of the road, and the back of the church." People certainly are funny. We are a bundle of ironies, inconsistencies and contradictions. Where we sit tells us lots about ourselves. It's comforting to know that we are at least on the bus, on the road and in the church!

Here's a word of warning: "Opportunity may only knock once, but temptation bangs on the door forever." This is only partly true. Temptation *is* always competing for our attention, but it's one of the things that keeps life interesting. Temptation is a lot like sports: It helps build character. Here's a word of warning: Don't be a person who can resist anything but temptation! Opportunity, however, happens more often than we think. The big challenge for us is to develop the eyes to see and the ears to hear the opportunities all around us.

One of the enjoyable things about one-liners is that they can encourage us to think of some of our own. Most of us love twists on the familiar and the trite. We love puns and word games. Here is one that spilled out of my brain: "Don't let the undertaker get the best and the rest of you. That part of you belongs to God."

Here's another one: "I've seen some ugly babies but never one whose mother and grandmother doesn't love it." Truth is, I've never seen an ugly baby — only beautiful little gifts from God.

Speaking of such gifts, Debi Nelson is one of those beautiful servants of God who works at Florence Crittenton Services in Charlotte, North Carolina. The organization assists single mothers with an opportunity for a healthy pregnancy, a healthy baby and a positive life. I love those people. My closing one-liner is one for you: "I love you too!" ✦

70

*P*risoners of Hope

I was invited to speak at a ministry where men spend four weeks in a residential program to fight addictions to drugs and alcohol. The program is supported by churches and interested donors who want to do something good for people caught in the grip of powerful forces that rob them of the freedom to be all that they can be. I used a theme suggested by a phrase from Zechariah 9:12 in which the Lord announces to the people of Zion that he is going to restore them to freedom. He calls them "prisoners of hope" and promises to restore to them double.

It's a powerful idea and seemed to me to be pertinent to folk who had entered a rehabilitation program in which they surrender some of their liberty for several weeks in order to escape a larger prison created by their addictions. They were voluntarily confined because they hoped for a better life. What's not to admire about men like that? So I asked if any of the men would like to offer a personal testimony about what it is like to be a prisoner. Several spoke about the tyranny of drug addiction. They were fine-looking men, black and white, young and middle-aged. They were very articulate and spoke from their own tragic experience.

One man, perhaps in his mid-40s, raised his hand and said, "I spent 27 years in prison." All eyes fell on him. He softly told a bit of his story to a rapt audience and commented about how important faith was becoming to him in his quest for freedom from addiction. Other men in the room murmured their identification with his journey.

To press my point, I told of my own experience as a volunteer teacher of creative writing behind the walls of the state penitentiary in Tennessee. I told them about the challenge I faced in getting inmates to write about what they knew. I wanted them to learn to face the truth.

What I observed was that the men who had committed horrendous crimes against women wanted to write romantic poems and stories glorifying girlfriends or mothers or wives. It was striking how often the prisoners idealized women in their writing even though they had beaten, raped and murdered women. So I encouraged the men to write what they knew, avoid denial and write what is true. Slowly but surely they began to do that and their writing became believable and good.

Eventually one of the men experienced the joy of having a book manuscript accepted for publication. He could not contain his pride and pleasure, but he would not allow me to read his manuscript. He knew I was a clergyman and finally confessed he had written a pornographic book. I never read his book, but I celebrated with him anyhow. I gave him an A+ in the course for practicing what I had been preaching about writing what you know.

When I finished my sermon and the service was over at the addictions program, the man who had spent 27 years in prison wanted to speak privately with me. He said, "I think I might write down my story." I encouraged him to do it. "It will be good for you, and it might help others as well. I would enjoy reading your story. Please do it." Then he left along with the other men. Moments later, when I walked out to my car to drive home, he was standing in the parking lot, waiting for me with a last word.

"Sir," he said, "I ain't never cared much for the Methodists, but that was the best sermon I ever heard." I roared with laughter and said, "Sir, that is the best compliment I've ever received." Then he and I shook hands, "God blessed" each other and we, *prisoners of hope*, said, "Good night." ✦

71

$\mathcal{R}$epaint and See-in No More

I'm worrying these days about all the people who have moved to the Southland and are ill prepared, without the most rudimentary tools, for getting along in this part of the country. So today the "Southern-Fried Perfesser" is giving a lecture on understanding Southern-Friedness.

In the first place, in order to live in the South, you need to be an astute judge of people. This is true whether you are evaluating a preacher or a politician — it's all the same. You can tell you are dealing with a levelheaded feller if his chewing tobacco drips out of *both* sides of his mouth. I learned this basic principle as a teenage Lothario. It's also a good way to evaluate a potential sweetheart.

In the second place, you must learn to understand Southern expressions of religion. And in the third place, you can't do that without grasping Southern pronunciations of common words. A lot of Southern-Friedness is preserved in the religious ideas, behavior and accents of our language. So, in the interest of brevity (which seldom applies to either religion or speech in the South), I will wrap these two topics into one ball of wax. Take a look at this list of stuff you can easily find all over the Southland:

> 1. Bubba has a fish (ancient Christian symbol) on both the bumper of his pickup truck *and* the butt of his assault rifle.

2. Billy Bob pronounces it: "Bab-tist."

3. Sister Sue Ann pronounces it: "Pull-pee-it."

4. The saintliest cook in the church always brings the tastiest deviled eggs to the church suppers.

5. People often pray so long before a meal, the food gets cold.

6. People in the South call Israel the "Holy Land."

7. Even in some large cities, people still honor funeral processions.

The plain truth is that we are losing a lot of our distinctive Southern accent at an alarming rate. It's because we're listening to too much radio and watching too much television, where a generic accent is spoken. What a relief when you hear somebody pronounce "sin" with two syllables —"see-in." You then know you're listening to a Southern-Fried somebody. Some folk think it's a "see-in" to laugh in church. Those same folk tend not to laugh much anywhere else either. The Lord is rumored to be puzzled by this.

It's true we have some pretty nutty religious ideas down here in the South that we need to "git shed of." (That's a Southern-Friedism that means "shuck off." Which means "git rid of.") And there's a bunch of behavior inside and outside the church that is just not right for decent, civilized people to do. But all right-thinking, religious people know that the first step toward *doing* right and *getting* right with God is to "repaint" and "see-in" no more.

That's what we've got to do. I'm as serious as a heart attack about this. ✦

72

1.4 *Degrees* of Misery

It's hot as… Well, you pick your own word to make the point of how this weather is affecting you. A Presbyterian preacher made his a one-sentence sermon the Sunday the mercury hit 100 degrees and the church's air conditioner failed. He proclaimed, "Sinners, if you think this is hot, just you wait!" Then he gave the benediction.

Our current heat wave has me pondering another of God's mysteries. We human beings are created to generally have a normal body temperature of 98.6 degrees. Why is it, then, that an additional 1.4 degrees makes us so gosh-darned miserable? How does that make sense? And for old geezers like me, this degree and a half is downright dangerous.

Oh, there are a few advantages to this sweltering heat. Watermelon tastes better on days like this and homemade ice cream is never better. But, on balance, I can do without this heat. Before we know it, we will be seeing armadillos, Gila monsters and alligators migrating up into these parts. I think the next time I hear somebody arguing that there is no such thing as global warming, I'll put some kind of curse on him.

I reckon something like this 1.4 degrees of misery has a lot to do with context. In a few months we will have temperatures in the teens. Our cheerful weather forecasters will appear on our screens and gleefully announce, "Well, folks, it's 14 degrees at the airport now, but take heart! By three o'clock this afternoon we will reach our high for the day, 15.4 degrees! Stay tuned for reports at the top of each hour." But when the 1.4 degrees takes us to 100, we go nuts — and for very good reason.

There was a time when a fellow could just leave off his long woolen underwear and his shoes. He'd pull on his bibbed overalls, leave them unbuttoned down the sides, put on his straw hat and go to work. Sartorial correctness won't allow that nowadays.

It really doesn't matter how high the heat is in the shade when you're all soggy around the gizzard in love with your beloved.

Still, I can think of times when 1.4 degrees of heat is anything but miserable. It really doesn't matter how high the heat is in the shade when you're all soggy around the gizzard in love with your beloved. You cuddle up to the other 98.6 degree bundle of body heat and it's okay — better than okay.

The motto of this divine column is "*Southern-Fried Preacher, a bit of what's Southern, fried or preachy and more or less fit to print.*" Well, I'm here to tell you, I'm living up to my slogan these days. I'm certainly fried. This time of summer is especially hard on preachers. For one thing, it makes people sleepier on Sunday mornings. Y'all come in and sit down in your padded pews, tired from the week you've had and overheated from walking from your car. You soon begin to nod off. Now, I'm the kind of preacher who is like an old soldier and waits to fire until he sees the whites of your eyes. I like to orate while looking at the whites of the congregation's eyes.

Your eyelids begin to creep down. Sleep is settling in. Your eyelids now begin to drift back up. Your head rocks back and I'm staring up your nostrils. Your eyeballs roll back into your skull — and *all* I can see now are the whites of your eyes! Then a terrible thing happens to me. I look at the serenity that seems to have come over you. I think, "How good it is to see someone resting so well — as if in the arms of God." Then I begin to get sleepy myself!

It's hard to be a preacher in a summer like this. However, I think I have a solution. I'm going to see if I can change from being a Methodist and become a Baptist for the month of August. And I think I'll do nothing but baptisms while I'm a Baptist parson. You know, we Methodists usually baptize by putting a few drops of water on the baptizee's head. Baptist preachers walk down into the water and immerse the candidate completely in the pool. I not only *can* do that — I *have* done it lots of times. It all depends on the context! ✦

73

𝒻ast Stuff

This is the Age of Rapidity. Fast food, rapid transit, high-speed Internet service: what's not to like about time-saving gadgets and convenient services? I was visiting a parishioner last week who had undergone surgery. She was making a rapid recovery and was soon to be discharged from the hospital. I remarked that if things continue apace, soon we will begin experiencing drive-thru surgeries.

Her sister, visiting from a large Southern city, told me about a drive-thru mortuary where she and her husband live. She asked that her hometown not be identified because it is becoming the object of unflattering publicity anyway. There are, she said, bad and bizarre goings-on. This Seven Eleven-type funeral home has a drive-by window where the deceased is placed on display in what is a very loose variation on the concept of window-shopping. Also, if viewers wish to leave condolences for the surviving relatives, written notes may be dropped in a box.

Driven by convenience-conscious consumers, churches are becoming more innovative all the time. A few years ago I heard about a priest who had installed a drive-thru confessional in his parish. As I understand it, a sinner could drive up, bare his soul and drive off to have a nice day unencumbered by unresolved guilt. I heard that the slogan for this ministry was "Toot-N-Tell or Go to Hell." I never knew whether this was a true report or simply an apocryphal tale.

Speaking of innovation, necessity is often the mother of invention in church life. When I was a young pastor, still in school but serving a tiny rural church, a ministerial buddy of mine, who was also a student-pastor, solved a Sunday morning crisis with imagination. He arrived at church one morning only to discover that there was no grape juice on hand for Holy Communion.

Fortunately, there was a small grocery in the village that was open early on Sundays. It was an era in which "blue laws" forbidding businesses to open before noon on Sundays were just beginning to be stricken from the books in most Southern communities. While this young theologian had made quite a reputation for himself in his town by giving rousing sermons condemning this new encroachment by commerce on the sanctity of the Sabbath, he breathed a prayer of gratitude as he drove to the grocery.

"Harold," he recounted to me later that week, "I was so relieved as I sheepishly walked into the store that morning to buy some grape juice to save the day. However, I searched the shelves to no avail. Then I asked the grocer if she had any juice. She shook her head in the negative. I asked if she might have any homemade wine, blackberry, elderberry, anything. Nope, she shook her head. Any hard cider?"

Drama mounted as I listened to this tale of impending woe. I asked, "Well, what did you do?"

"Finally there was nothing left to do. The grocer stirred around in the cooler and withdrew for me what she said was the closest thing she had to what I needed. She handed me a Dr. Pepper and saved the day!"

Last Sunday at First United Methodist Church in Gastonia, we discovered a shortage of bread just before the early service. Sheriff Leroy Russell, who for more than 20 years has been an usher at the church, jumped into his car and raced to the nearest grocery. He was back in a flash with a beautiful loaf of bread. We had what I'm calling a "blue light special" Communion service. ✦

74

$\mathcal{T}$he Required Chapter

No book like this can close without a chapter like this. I want to tell you a bit about my family.

I take enormous pleasure in my entire extended family. We are beginning to learn lots about our ancestors thanks to a cousin who has become a family historian. I'm not going to delve into that except to say that my mother's side of the family is named Harless. My wife's family names were Byrd and Rose. Maybe one of you, dear readers, will share such family names and be able to educate me. I hope this book will fall into the hands of some cousins I have not known. What I want mostly to focus on are my siblings and children.

There are four of us siblings. I am the eldest. My brother Steve is about 18 months younger than I. He got the brains for business in our family. He married Cheryl, who brought the genes for brains to their family. They have produced a wonderful brood of children who are brilliant, world-class intellects. Steve is characteristic of my siblings: generous to a fault, a great brother. My only conflict with him is over the fact that he always has to telephone me — I rarely call him. It isn't personal with him. I just have this thing about the telephone. I don't use it much.

Steve has a fine sense of humor, but he tends to be less bombastic than I. I guffaw; he chuckles. Not long ago he sent me a note to tell me he had been going through a box of documents left by our parents, who are both deceased. In the letter, he enclosed their marriage certificate and wrote, "Please note the date of their marriage and compare it to your own birthdate. This is conclusive proof that you are not the old bastard people think you are."

I fell onto the floor with laughter. That is the funniest thing he has ever said. When I told him I was putting together this book and intended to recount this episode, he didn't even remember it. However, he did confess he wanted me to send him a copy. He asked me to mark the page where this tale appears. He didn't want to have to read the whole thing to find the part about him! I'm telling this at the last so he will, in fact, need to read the whole thing. This will probably make this the first book he has read from cover to cover in 40 years!

The Bales brothers (l-r): Me and my brothers, Steve & Lynn

My sister's name is Brenda. Her story is heartbreaking. In her mid-30s she became a widow with a young son, Derek. Then when Derek was in his late teens, she disappeared. She is one of those hundreds of thousands of Americans who have simply disappeared. We have searched in every way we know, but to no avail. Still, we hope and pray that she is alive and will someday reappear. She was important glue helping hold our family together. She was the most generous person I have ever known. All year long she shopped for gifts to later give at Christmas or birthdays or other special family occasions. Family meant everything to her. Now Judy and I think of Derek, who is a professor of psychology at the University of New Mexico, as our own son. His wife, Brandi, is also a psychologist.

My baby brother is Lynn. He is in his 50s now, has a ponytail and a beard but is still my *baby* brother. He is a great musician and teacher, living in Turkey, where he works for the U.S. Defense Department. His wife, Mary, is a career military officer now assigned to the Pentagon in Washington. Their bright children live in the U.S. now, having grown up around the world as prototypical military brats. During my frequent health crises of the past several years, Lynn has often come from wherever he was assigned around the world to tend to me. It makes tears come to my eyes to think about his kindness.

In one generation, we rose from the ranks of working folk with modest educations to the affluent middle class.

Judy and I have four children. Janice, our first, died four years ago. Earlier in this book I have written about her — *Southern-Fried Daughter* and *A Different Kind of Tears.* Nothing hurts a parent's heart like the death of a child. She died on her 45th birthday. We miss her every day. She had a fabulous sense of humor, left us with many good memories and two wonderful grandchildren, John and Jenny White. They make us proud for the young adults they have become.

Our eldest son, David, is an artist with wood and with plants. He started his adult life selling investments but soon left that to eventually become a master woodworker. Last year he became a certified *luthier.* Now, I know you are asking, "What is a *luthier?*" It is a maker of stringed musical instruments — guitars, violins, lutes — things like that. He takes exotic woods and makes beautiful instruments out of them. As to artistry with plants, we were at his and his wife, Christie's, house yesterday and were dwarfed by his tomato plants. They stand at least eight feet tall! He gave us grandchildren, Shea and Wesley, who give us much joy.

Philip is our youngest son. He and his wife, Lisa, are our adventurers. They have twice ridden their Harley Davidson motorcycles from Charlotte, North Carolina, to Portland, Oregon, and back. They plan to live on a sailboat when their daughters finish college. Philip is a nuclear reactor operator. He is also my go-to person when I have computer problems. He has threatened that, if I mess up the new computer that he has just given me, he is going to permanently confiscate my mouse. Their daughters, Caitlyn and Megan, are a delight to us. In this book I have included an exchange of emails between Megan and me, entitled *Dudely Papaw.*

Susannah is our youngest child. I have written about her in several places earlier in this book. She was our surprise baby in our mid-40s, born 17 years after Philip, her nearest sibling. She is now a young adult, finishing a graduate degree at Emory University in Atlanta and planning to marry Patrick Faulhaber this autumn. We love Patrick! Susannah is a gifted speaker and writer. I wish I could write as well as she does!

I am blessed to have a wonderful family. We are one of those millions of American families that have a special distinction. In one generation, we rose from the ranks of working folk with modest educations to the affluent middle class. Now we have many college-educated members and lots of members who have doctoral degrees. I attribute this good fortune to our having had forebears who valued education, hard work, family loyalty, mutual support and spirituality. God has been good to us. America has been good to us. And we have done our best to be good for America. ✦

$\mathcal{H}$arold K. Bales

Motto: *A Bit of What's Southern, Fried or Preachy and More or Less Fit to Print.*

Harold Bales considers himself a very blessed man. He has spent more than half of his fifty years in ministry as a denominational executive in The United Methodist Church. Joining the staff of the General Board of Evangelism while in seminary allowed him a great opportunity to grow into a mature minister while working with and being mentored by many of the great leaders of world Christianity and visiting many nations as a lecturer, consultant and preacher. Harold's greatest joy has been his pastoral service in the local parish, which has provided a platform for his dedication and quest for social justice, civil rights, education and ministry to the poor.

Now in semi-retirement, writing for publication occupies most of Harold's time. Throughout his career, he has written and edited many books. For twenty years he has pursued a public ministry beyond the walls of the church by writing a weekly newspaper column, "The Southern-Fried Preacher."

This pursuit began shortly after the death of his mother, Edith. For his own grief process and to pay tribute to his mother, Harold wrote about her descent into Alzheimer's disease and put it in a personal newsletter. Using the name "The Southern-Fried Preacher" for the newsletter came from a suggestion made by Terry Mattingly, former Religion Editor of *The Charlotte Observer*. Mattingly, now a syndicated columnist for Scripps Howard News Service, had noted the occasional op-ed pieces Harold had contributed to *The Observer* and suggested he write a regular newspaper column and name it "The Southern-Fried Preacher."

The first "Southern-Fried Preacher" went out to 35 family and friends. In it he mentioned he would send out another newsletter whenever he had something else to say and it would be free, but only those who asked for it would receive it. Kays Gary, legendary journalist in the region, got hold of the newsletter and reprinted it in his column. As a result, the second issue went to more than 2,000 readers and the third grew to beyond 4,000. Harold bought a secondhand copy machine to print the, now monthly, free newsletter. Family and friends volunteered to help label and prepare it for mailing. Readers began to send small donations to help pay for postage; some sent stamps.

Eight years later, the newsletter morphed into a weekly newspaper column and the name "The Southern-Fried Preacher" stuck. Remaining down-home, witty, sometimes preachy and sometimes cranky — in a good-natured sort of way — he regards the column as a weekly word for a bunch of good friends.

Harold loves plain talk, pooh-poohs political correctness and believes humorlessness is a serious heresy. He considers himself pious, but not pietistic. His writing has created a wide circle of friends to include those from Christian denominations and non-Christian faiths, as well as atheists, agnostics and religious skeptics. He says, "Like the late humorist Will Rogers and often-married actress Elizabeth Taylor, I never met a man I didn't like."

Harold describes himself as a garden-variety Methodist and a progressive, evangelical Christian. He admits this baffles some but makes perfect sense to him: "I'm happy to leave it to God to figure all that out at the end." ✦

The Bales Family

Shea & Wesley

Dave & Christie

Jenny

John

Lisa, Megan, Caity & Phil

Patrick & Susannah

Get Southern-Fried Every Day!

The Southern-Fried Preacher will email to you a
"Daily Nugget" of his wit, wisdom and sanctified silliness.

The Daily Nugget

You can be Southern-Fried no matter where you live. Everyone lives south of somewhere. It's all a matter of the heart.

Join My Mailing List

The Daily Nugget

Sign up at www.thesouthernfriedpreacher.com

What readers are saying …

"Harold Bales has just taken his wit and wisdom to another level with his daily email message, The Daily Nugget."

"Thanks for sending these. I love them!"

"I love this man!! Have subscribed so I can read regularly!"

"The Nuggets just start my day in a great way."

"I did such joyful laughter that I almost tipped out of my chair."

"Your wonderful articles give us something to think about and keep us laughing."

"Several of our friends are signing up."

"I have been enjoying your little Daily Nuggets. May we post them on the church website? I've always believed it's important to pass along a good thing to others!"

"He looks like everyone's granddaddy. I love him already. Give him a kiss from me."

"What a good thing you did, my friend. Thanks for sharing such a "keeper.""

Sign Up Now … The Daily Nugget Is Free!!
www.thesouthernfriedpreacher.com